Dynamic Stewardship Strategies

Dynamic Stewardship Strategies

Harnessing Time, Talent,
and Treasury
for Church Growth

George E. Brazell

BAKER BOOK HOUSE
Grand Rapids, Michigan 49516

Copyright 1989 by Baker Book House Company

ISBN: 0-8010-0971-5

Printed in the United States of America

Scripture quotations are from the King James Version of the Bible.

To
Anna Foster Brazell
and
Elinor Ruth Fowler

Faithful stewards
who made valuable contributions
to this book.

Contents

    Preface   9
1. A Scriptural Basis for Stewardship   11
2. The Christian Philosophy of Stewardship   21
3. A Christian's Value System   37
4. The Stewardship of Personal Capabilities   53
5. The Christian Steward's Organizational Plan   65
6. Implementing Church Stewardship   79
7. Stewardship and the Tithe   91
8. Stewards in the Home   105
9. Stewards in the Community   119
10. Stewards in the World   133

Preface

It is my firm conviction that believers in the gospel should "Christianize" all the processes of daily living. Being a Christian here and now sustains the hope that the kingdom of God will soon come and that his will may be done "in earth as it is in heaven."

I propose to examine the work of the church as carried out by its organizations, its education arms, and its members as individuals. There are almost as many types of local church situations as there are clergy and lay individuals within the church universal. The strength of the church lies in both its divine origin and its ministry of the inspired Word. All members are called to be stewards of time, talent, and treasury.

George Brazell

1

A Scriptural Basis for Stewardship

Definition of Stewardship

Stewardship has meant different things to different people. A very early use of the term *steward* was to describe a person hired to care for pigs. Later, the term was applied to anyone who managed the property of another.

Today "steward" can have various meanings, too. An airline steward cares for the needs of passengers. On board a ship a steward waits on tables, attends to the staterooms, or serves the passengers in a variety of other ways. The term *steward* can also refer to a manager, a supervisor, or an administrator. Each definition carries the basic thought that a steward's services are not rendered to satisfy his (or her) own needs. Stewardship means working on behalf of someone else, and stewards benefit from their labors only indirectly.

Some people mistakenly limit the meaning of stewardship to monetary concerns. They faithfully place into the church treasury 10 percent of their incomes and feel they have done their part to spread the gospel and thus maintained their faithfulness as stewards. But stewardship relates to more than just one's material possessions.

Rather, stewardship is the sum total of our attitude and reaction toward the divine Creator and his creation. God, the maker of all creation, is Landlord of earth and sky—and man is the responsible servant entrusted with and commissioned to implement God's program on earth so as to fulfill the Creator's divine plan.

Stewardship in the Old Testament

In the Old Testament, stewardship dealt mainly with the management of domestic affairs on the national, family, and personal levels. For example, Moses was designated by God as the person responsible for the administration and proper leadership in all the affairs of Israel and its people. A more specific illustration is found on the list of Solomon's officials and officers: Ahishar was placed in charge of the palace (1 Kings 4:6).

The Sovereign Creator

The Old Testament believers held to the basic idea that Jehovah-God was sovereign, that he owned all creation. The Genesis account of creation teaches God's sovereignty, and Israel's devotional literature shows they accepted the teaching as authoritative. The writer of the Psalms emphasized this point when he wrote, "The earth is the LORD's, and the fulness thereof; the world, and they that dwell therein" (24:1). God was claiming rightful ownership when he said, ". . . whatsoever is under the whole heaven is mine" (Job 41:11). He defined the extent of his authority when he uttered, "The heaven is my throne, and the earth is my footstool . . ." (Isa. 66:1). There was no question in a true Israelite's mind as to the ownership of *any* parcel of ground. God had clearly pointed this out in Leviticus 25:23: ". . . for the land is mine; for ye are strangers and sojourners with

A Scriptural Basis for Stewardship

me." Belief in God as sovereign Creator places man subject to him in all things.

The Chosen People

The Old Testament is a direct message from God to Israel, his chosen people. God's choice of Israel is clearly set forth in Scripture: "Now therefore, if ye will obey my voice indeed, and keep my covenant, then ye shall be a peculiar treasure unto me above all people; for all the earth is mine: And ye shall be unto me a kingdom of priests, and an holy nation . . ." (Exod. 19:5–6).

The relationship of Israel to God as his "treasure" and of God to Israel as their sovereign and holy ruler was deeply impressed upon the Israelites' memories by their deliverance out of Egyptian bondage. The writer of the Book of Deuteronomy expressed this in no uncertain terms:

> For thou art an holy people unto the LORD thy God: the LORD thy God hath chosen thee to be a special people unto himself, above all people that are upon the face of the earth. The LORD did not set his love upon you, nor choose you, because ye were more in number than any people; for ye were the fewest of all people: But because the LORD loved you, and because he would keep the oath which he had sworn unto your fathers, hath the LORD brought you out with a mighty hand, and redeemed you out of the house of bondmen, from the hand of Pharaoh king of Egypt *(Deut. 7:6–8)*.

God formed this body of former slaves into a nation. He took these wanderers and established them in a land of promise and plenty. In his infinite love and mercy, God selected Israel to be his people: "And I will take you to me for a people, and I will be to you a God, and ye shall know that I am the LORD your God . . ." (Exod. 6:7).

Property Regulations

Even though private ownership was acknowledged in principle, there were some general regulations about property that every Israelite was expected to follow (see Lev. 25). One of the most prominent of these regulations concerned the so-called sabbatical year. After land had been cultivated six consecutive years, it was to remain fallow for one year, this being an attempt to give back to the earth a portion of that which had been taken from it. The Sabbath of Sabbaths, or year of jubilee, provided that every fifty years the Israelites would further show their belief in God's sovereignty by observance of several other special rulings. In this way they would accept their role as stewards, not owners, underscoring that they considered *God* the ultimate Owner of all land.

Israelite property holders achieved protection of their rights by living in accordance with God's law. For example, Deuteronomy 19:14 contains a prohibition against the removal of a neighbor's landmark, and removing a marker was considered a very serious offense (see Deut. 27:17). The Ten Commandments told Israel that all thievery was frowned upon (Deut. 5:19) and that even coveting a neighbor's property was forbidden (v. 21). Needless to say, these prohibited practices clearly violate the principle of stewardship because in effect they deny God's sovereign ownership of *everything*. Stealing the possessions of another is equivalent to stealing from God.

Old Testament Stewards

God gave Adam the world and all that was in it except for one thing—the special tree in the midst of the Garden of Eden. Adam was to manage God's world and oversee what took place in it. But God, by placing off limits "the

A Scriptural Basis for Stewardship

tree of knowledge of good and evil" showed that he was the true owner of all the things he had created. Adam was, in reality, God's steward. When Adam disobeyed God's prohibition about that tree, he transgressed the principles of stewardship and was branded a sinner.

Abraham, on the other hand, had an attitude altogether different from that of Adam. Whereas Adam supposed that whatever he could grasp was his own, Abraham reasoned that all he possessed really belonged to God. Thus, when God gave Abraham victory over his enemies and helped him rescue his loved ones, Abraham acknowledged God as "the most high God, the possessor of heaven and earth" (Gen. 14:22). This is the principle of stewardship in action.

When the people of Israel acknowledged God's ownership of all things by tithing of all they managed as his stewards, they were actually giving their substance in support of their religious leaders, the Levites. But this did not end the chain of stewardship responsibilities. The Levites themselves acted as stewards by tithing of what they received, recognizing by this act God's true ownership of all things. Throughout the Old Testament accounts, men of faith did not consider themselves as owning their possessions, but rather as managing them in the capacity of stewards of God's property.

Stewardship in the New Testament

God is the Author of stewardship. Although he gave the Old Testament believers the original principle of stewardship, that concept carries right into the New Testament era. Some people mistakenly hold firmly to the idea that stewardship is merely an old Jewish custom and thus is not part of the Christianity of the New Testament. In reality, stewardship is the very essence of Christianity. Just as to be a Christian is to put God first, to practice stewardship is to put God first. The basic question an individual must consider when faced with a challenge to exercise Christian stewardship is whether any Christian can afford *not* to put God first in his or her life.

When an individual has accepted Christ as Savior, that person has also accepted the responsibility of living by Christ's teachings. Christians have confessed Christ. They have promised to be disciples of Christ. Their names are listed on the church membership record. Can any among that body of believers afford to deny the Lord any part of their being? To do so is to lead a life of selfishness, the very contradiction of New Testament stewardship principles.

The Teachings of Jesus

So far as we know, Jesus did not leave any writings. Most of what we know about his teachings is found in the four Gospels. These accounts were written by men who believed that Jesus Christ was the Son of God. His birth, his life, his ministry, his teachings, his crucifixion, his resurrection, his ascension—everything he did and believed—substantiated their conviction in his divinity. Christ, the Son of God, taught men how to live in right relationship with the Father. His teachings clearly reveal to us stewardship as he wanted his disciples and all other believers to practice it.

The Strange World of the Gospels. When beginning a study of the Gospels, one is unmistakably guided by a group of men who recognized the sovereignty of God. These men stood out in sharp relief against a background of Greco-Roman humanism. The pagan world around them glorified and even worshiped man and his accomplishments. But for one group of stalwart men, God dominated everything. They came to see God as

A Scriptural Basis for Stewardship

Maker, Sustainer, sovereign Lord, and eternal Judge. As Head of all nations, God directs all creation and works miracles. He gives life, for God is Life. These men, who believed that God was and is sovereign forever, knew God best as Jesus Christ, Son of man and Son of God.

The Strange Person of the Gospels. The Son of God in many ways showed that he had power over all things, including sometimes disregarding the traditions of the Jews by healing on the Sabbath. In doing this, Jesus claimed that he was Lord even of the Sabbath (Mark 2:28). The healing itself showed his sovereignty over affliction and disease.

When Jesus healed the man lowered to him through the roof of a house, he restored the man to proper health and declared that the man's sins were forgiven—though no one but God can forgive sins. Yet Christ forgave because he is God, and he is sovereign!

Jesus rebuked the temple merchants for desecrating that sacred place. By overturning the tables of money-changers, and driving out those who sold animals for sacrifice, he proved his authority in his Father's house.

That small group who came to believe totally in God's sovereignty was the band of humble men who followed Christ. He taught them the way to live, and he did it mainly by example. Jesus' ideal for right living can be seen in his attitude toward his own life, which was that his life was not his alone. He had come to do the will of his Father. This is the heart of Christ's teaching about stewardship. He thought of himself as a servant and knew that his life was not his to manage. It was a trust from God, to be used for the glory of God.

The Believer-Steward. The Lord Jesus Christ submitted himself to the status of a servant. The disciple cannot be greater than the Master. From the biblical viewpoint, man owns nothing, not even his life. All things belong to God. Yet we see from Christ's life—as from the lives of the Old and New Testament saints—that God wants us to buy and sell, to work and play, to share the normal responsibilities of life. But we are to do all these things mindful of our ongoing role as stewards of God.

Since whatever we possess we receive as gifts from God, it is our duty to use those gifts according to his will and for his glory. Even the way we use our time is to depend on what God wants us to do. As Christian believers, we are called upon to manage all the affairs of daily life as stewards of God. Jesus has taught us that God is sovereign and that to do God's will is the highest duty of man. This is Christian stewardship.

The Steward and His Possessions. Wealth is neither good nor evil within itself, for sin dwells not in lifeless coins but within human hearts. Riches may be either a blessing or a curse. Many times, those who have riches turn away from God because they are too preoccupied with material things. But a poor man may be just as unrighteous as a wealthy one. He may be obsessed with a desire for possessions and filled with bitterness because of the things he lacks. Conversely, a man with wealth and worldly goods may be as righteous as a man who owns practically nothing.

The Bible warns against amassing a fortune for fortune's sake. People sometimes allow possessions to hinder their relations with God, for—in Jesus' words: "... where your treasure is, there will your heart be also" (Matt. 6:21).

Jesus did have a proper respect for property, however. Roman authority levied taxes for the support of the government, and Jesus did not refuse to acknowledge the necessity for taxes. His desire to conform to civic regulations was surpassed only by his desire to please God.

A Scriptural Basis for Stewardship

Jesus set a perfect example of stewardship by using all he had, including his very life, to do God's will. And he teaches us to do the same. Although earthly possessions may receive earthly respect and recognition, the sovereign God rules all things, both temporal and eternal, and we are only his servants.

Stewardship According to Paul

The apostle Paul launched a program of active stewardship when he appealed to the church at Corinth to relieve the suffering "saints" at Jerusalem (see 1 Cor. 16:1–3; cf. 2 Cor. 8:1–4). To encourage the liberality of the growing body of Christians, he suggested they receive an offering. Because of the great distress of other believers, it was needful that the Corinthian brethren act immediately. The pressing need gave the church at Corinth an opportunity to exercise the Christian gesture of giving, to share in "the fellowship of the ministering to the saints" (2 Cor. 8:4).

In one of Paul's letters to Timothy, a sound basis is given not only for stewardship practices, but also for all the functions within the church of God (1 Tim. 6:17–19). Paul warned Timothy against any teacher who would not agree with the words of Jesus (2 Tim. 4:3–5). Jesus' words alone would lead to righteous living, and a stewardship emphasis should flow naturally from the knowledge of the teachings of Jesus.

Paul pointed out in much of his writing that life in this world is for preparing to live beyond the grave. He reminded us in 1 Timothy 6:7 that we brought nothing into the world and cannot take anything out of it. Most of us are well aware of this fact, but so few act according to its wisdom!

Throughout his letters, Paul expressed his own view of Christian stewardship, including the idea that family as well as individual property ownership also carries a stewardship responsibility. Paul discourages thriftlessness in his letters to the church at Thessalonica. He insists that if one refused to work, he should not eat (2 Thess. 3:10). An irresponsible attitude is never acceptable in the sight of God.

Paul realized the possibility of misinterpreting the idea that godliness is "great gain" (1 Tim. 6:6). Love of money can be the root of many evils (see v. 10), but getting rid of money would not rid the world of evil. The evil roots ensnare the rebellious hearts of individuals who refuse to conform to the will of God and acknowledge his sovereignty.

Timothy was instructed to aim at righteousness, faith, steadfastness, love, godliness, and gentleness if he was to be a true steward of Jesus Christ. He was to shun wrong attitudes toward worldly possessions. Paul had known those who, for the love of owning, had wandered from God. But there was a higher and more noble cause to which Timothy was to pledge his allegiance. He was to "fight the good fight of faith" (1 Tim. 6:12)—be humble, do good, trust in the Lord, spread the gospel, minister to the needs of others, and lay hold on life eternal. Paul could never have given Timothy a greater charge. It is the basic call to Christian stewardship, and it is the call that comes now to all believers in Christ and his gospel.

The Christian Philosophy of Stewardship

Stewardship in the Early Church

Jesus commissioned the early church, and the church of today as well, to preach the gospel to every kindred, tongue, and nation. To accomplish this work, God presented the plan of Christian stewardship, a program that *he* designed, just as he designed all phases of Christian religious expression. Similarly, when the Lord established a system of worship among his chosen people, he did not leave it to the imaginations of men. Nothing about the one true religion came into the world by chance. It was planned by God.

When the wilderness tabernacle of the Israelites was erected, it was built according to God's plan. Moses had learned all the details while on Mount Sinai talking with God. Later, when Solomon's glorious temple replaced the wilderness tabernacle, that magnificent yet functional temple was not an outgrowth of the king's superior architectural knowledge. Rather, God had given David the blueprints, and David had passed them on to Solomon (1 Chron. 28).

As in the past, our Lord has passed on to his Church of today his plan for reaching the goals he has set before it. Let us therefore now examine God's plan for achieving worldwide Christianity as it was revealed in the early church.

Ministering to the Saints

After Christ's ascension, some of the believers found themselves in serious financial need. But, since they generally were "of one heart and of one soul . . . they had all things [in] common. . . . And distribution was made unto every man according as he had need" (Acts 4:32, 35). Although many in the early church had left their homes and even their families to follow Christ's leading, Christians met the needs of the less fortunate. The church thereupon elected seven men to care for the needy (Acts 6). This appears as one of the first recorded incidents of the early church's ministering to the physical needs of the saints as distinct from its spiritual ministry.

A later incident also involved the Jerusalem church, which was going through a difficult period because a famine had hit the area. Then the needs of the dependent members were met because Paul persuaded the Gentile churches in Macedonia, Achaia, and Galatia to provide for the poorer members of the church in Judea. Paul wrote to the Galatians: "So then, as we have opportunity, let us do good to all men, especially to those who are of the household of faith" (6:10). In those words we can see Paul's recognition of Jesus' teaching about helping those in need. Jesus had clearly informed his followers that if they clothed the naked, fed the hungry, and visited those in prison, they would be ministering unto him (Matt. 25:35–46).

The Christian Philosophy of Stewardship 23

Furthering the Gospel

A ministry of relieving human suffering through material generosity is an essential factor in the elements of Christian giving, but Paul touched on an even stronger note. He wrote (probably while "detained" in Rome) and thanked the church at Philippi for the assistance they had given him by sending their gifts (Phil. 4:16–18) and, more specifically, for the furtherance of the gospel (1:5).

Paul knew that a vital portion of the gospel had been assigned to him. He realized that he had been commissioned to proclaim to all men the message of forgiveness from God. Those who supported Paul, including his fellow ministers, shared in this ministry around the world.

Becoming Rich in Good Deeds

When an individual dedicates a portion of his or her wealth to the cause of Christ, that person has the satisfaction of knowing that this pleases the Master. Paul emphasized to Timothy the necessity for commanding those who have possessions that they must share with those who have not—to be "rich in good deeds" (1 Tim. 6:17–18). But goodness must spring from an inward desire, must begin within and work outward.

Wrong motives for giving detract from the overall virtue of Christian concern. Perhaps the lowest motive for so-called generosity is an attempt to bribe God. Such donors bring their gifts, which may or may not be "sacrificial," with the hope that they might induce God to treat them favorably or refrain from harming them. This hardly is Christian stewardship!

One excellent motive for "good deeds" is worldwide evangelism. This causes many to give liberally. All

Christians should share in the support of worldwide evangelism, whether it is city missions—going across the street to win a soul to Christ; or state missions—going across the state for that purpose; home missions—going across the continent to spread the gospel; or foreign missions—going across the ocean in response to Christ's calling. Spiritual needs are met through this giving, but so are social, family, and physical concerns and suffering in all areas of life daily.

Perhaps the strongest motive for giving is the love for others that God puts in the heart of the born-again Christian. Giving is inseparable from one's new nature in Christ. The true believer loves God, and God's Word. It follows that he or she loves God's people and loves to spread the gospel. A Christian's greatest joy comes from helping others find the same kind of total fulfillment.

Reaching All for Christ

Some people act as if the gospel is only for a specific group of people, those "on trial" for their lives. But rich or poor, learned or ignorant, pious or depraved—all people stand before God with an equal opportunity to accept the gift of salvation. The most important thing anyone can do in life is to lay hold of eternity. Our days on earth are so short, fading like a vapor, a shadow, the grass of the field, a summer flower. Life eternal is a different matter: it is for always.

Paul admonished Timothy to charge believers to "lay hold on eternal life" (1 Tim. 6:19), to remind everyone, as Jesus taught, that only storing "treasures in heaven" can lead to eternal security (e.g., Matt. 6:19–20).

No one should think money can be used to buy the rights to life eternal. Salvation comes only as a gracious gift from God. It is true, however, that individuals may express the depth of their response to God by the genuineness of their stewardship. Handling our stewardship as God intended will enable us to face the end of life in this world with the hope of taking hold of life eternal, the only true life.

Goals of a Christian

Paul urged Timothy to "follow righteousness, faith, charity, peace, with them that call on the Lord out of a pure heart" (2 Tim. 2:22). What greater goal could today's Christian set than the one placed before Timothy so long ago?

On the fringes of Christianity wander many who allow their materialistic craving for possessions to lead them away from fellowship with God. Certainly, Christians must to some degree think about their property, income, and satisfying vocations. But all these concerns should be illuminated by the light of God's purpose. To omit God's will for one's life, when setting goals and making plans, will lead only to disaster. The noble goals Paul told Timothy to pursue are among the most important graces of Christian living and should be the goals of every Christian.

Agreement with the Lord

Stated in its simplest terms, Christianity is a philosophy of love—the love of God for man and of man for God. Implicit in this concept is the love of man for man. Jesus said in language very plain and easy to understand, "By this shall all men know that ye are my disciples, if ye have love one to another" (John 13:35).

If the chief purpose in someone's life is to pile up earthly treasure, that goal will not be a secret very long. If a man is more concerned with what he owns than with God and his fellowman, his wrongly placed love will quickly come to light. Those who are ready to trade eternal principles for worldly profits make their preference obvious. They are always known by their heavenly Father and usually by other people as well in the long run.

If the goal of the strong man is to seize power, he will be seizing it at the expense of all others. And if a man's greatest desire is for applause, he will be found among the noisy and blatant, making superficial friendships designed to help him reach his goal of public affirmation.

But love of a man for God is expressed in the ongoing desire to do the will of God. When such a man has brought himself into agreement with the Lord's commands and purposes, his love toward other people will quickly follow. This agreement with the Lord automatically leads directly to a life of happy stewardship.

The Heart of Stewardship

In the distinction between ownership and possession lies the essence of the stewardship doctrine. The man who accepts that all possessions are actually the property of God, but are entrusted to human hands for administration, acknowledges that he is accountable to God for their use—not only for returning one-tenth, but also for the stewardship of the remaining nine-tenths.

This concept of possessions means that God is the Owner and his followers are stewards who administer or manage his affairs on earth. This makes a definite connection between earth-life and heaven-life. Proper (or improper) management of the earth-life determines whether heaven-life will be the final result.

Here is one of the most impressive facts of Hebrew history. During the time periods when the chosen people were most faithful in observing their religious vows and in maintaining their divine Father's faith, they were also the most prosperous and safest from attack from outside enemies. Ultimately, life on earth and in heaven will be directed generously by God for the faithful steward.

Spiritual Perils in Wrong Attitudes

When Solomon's domain divided into Israel (northern kingdom) and Judah (southern kingdom) the people of Israel were led astray by a king who undertook to make their religion "easy" for them. During the chaotic days that followed the northern kingdom's repudiation of the house of David and Judah's young King Rehoboam, a rebel cast-off named Jeroboam was called back from his self-imposed exile in Egypt to take the throne of the ten tribes of Israel.

While a fugitive from Solomon's court, Jeroboam had learned much about the worship of the people in the Nile Country.

Fearing that the annual visits of his people to the great temple in Jerusalem might result in a revived loyalty to the house of David, Jeroboam tried to overcome this natural trend by erecting golden calves at two popular shrines, Dan and Bethel. The idolatrous king insisted that the people no longer needed to go to Jerusalem, which was technically part of the rival kingdom of Judah. (See 1 Kings 12.)

Christians cannot bargain with God. They must give themselves in full surrender, yielding to service for the Lord with no thought of using him for their own purposes. If one thinks of "godliness" primarily as a way of gain—a means to a selfish end—he or she has completely misunderstood the Christian faith.

In the Christian experience, a dedicated believer is ready to suffer loss of all things and count them only as waste if through this he or she may gain Christ. (See Phil. 3:8.) Spiritual perils and chaos will surely develop from wrong attitudes.

Supporting the Christian Minister. Ministers are obligated by God's call to preach the whole counsel of God. Just as a minister must preach the Word of God that condemns the murderer, the thief, the liar, the drunkard, he is also called on to preach the Word that condemns the covetous, self-serving Christian.

When the Holy Spirit convicts a sinner of his or her covetousness, sometimes the sinner (instead of repenting) merely goes about resenting the messenger who has delivered the Word of God. The sinner would not think of fighting against God or God's Word so the minister-messenger receives the indignation of the sinner. Especially vulnerable is the minister who speaks out on the subject of tithing or giving. The covetous, self-serving person may rationalize by mentally rehearsing all the items a certain amount of money could buy for personal use rather than giving the amount to God's work.

Godliness and Contentment. In a modern industrialized society such as our own, money is something we can hardly live without! We need it for sheer survival—for food, clothing, and shelter and, increasingly, for education and training for our children and ourselves. Acquiring adequate income for our needs and to attain a reasonable sense of security is a universal goal and one not to be condemned *if* that is the basic motivation. The Christian who is content with the necessities of life has realized great gain—but the worship of money is a blot on society today.

No man is more unhappy than the one who is striving constantly to increase the size of his bank account. He will never be satisfied with his lot, even when he equals or exceeds the affluence level of his neighbors. In striving to get all from life that he thinks he deserves *materially*, a man always falls short of contentment.

A things-are-different-today-from-what-they-were-in-biblical-times attitude is no justification for blind materialism. Faith in God's provision is still the key to happiness. It took absolute faith in God to sustain the seventy disciples sent by Jesus on their first evangelistic tour. They went into unfriendly towns where the people were indifferent or hostile and the days were hard. Hunger, discomfort, hate, ridicule, scorn, and many other forms of adversity greeted them. They did not have nineteen centuries of experiences of the Christian faithful to reassure them. They had no finance committee whose chairman they could contact for supplies if things went wrong. But "the seventy returned again with joy" (Luke 10:17) because they had trusted God through it all.

Trusting God brings overall contentment in Christian living. It is when Christians launch out to follow the Lord's leading that his promises are fulfilled and contentment is achieved.

Witnessing the Good Confession. As Paul gradually resigned himself to the fact that he had reached the end of his journey in this life, he wrote to Timothy these words, "I have fought a good fight . . . I have kept the faith" (2 Tim. 4:7). Paul challenged his protégé to strive to do the same (vv. 1–5). Paul knew that the Christian's reward would come from having faithfully served the Lord.

A Christian's faithfulness is best seen by his or her deeds. Any man who could not be trusted with dimes would surely make a poor custodian of dollars. If a woman wastes minutes on her job, she would probably also waste hours elsewhere. A store clerk who would defraud an individual of a few cents would unquestionably be a dangerous risk where thousands of dollars were concerned. The citizen who does not respect a neighbor's property rights could hardly be trusted to respect human rights in general. Small things do count with God.

How Much Shall I Keep for Myself?

It has been suggested that 10 percent of the Christian world's church membership cannot be located; 20 percent seldom pray, 25 percent never read the Bible; 30 percent do not attend church; 40 percent give only a dime to the Lord's work per year; 50 percent never go to Sunday school; 60 percent never go to the Sunday evening service; 75 percent give only five cents per year to missions; 80 percent never go to prayer meeting; 90 percent do not have a family altar; and 95 percent have never won a soul to Christ. But the work of God must go on nevertheless.

Under Mosaic Law, giving was regulated for the Jews on the basis of tithes and offerings. According to the New Testament, Christian giving, which is based on love, should surpass the Old Testament requirements. Before an individual answers the question, "How much shall I keep for myself?" there are five "if's" that should be considered:

1. If I give nothing, I am voting to close the doors of my church, disobeying God, and thereby suggesting that other church members do the same.
2. If I give only to current expenses, I am voting against missions and Christian education and disobeying the Great Commission to take the gospel to the ends of the earth.
3. If I give grudgingly and only when pressured, I will miss the joy of giving; I will not be a cheerful giver.

The Christian Philosophy of Stewardship 31

4. If I refuse to give on a regular basis, I am not seeking first the kingdom of God.
5. If I give only what I think is "required," I am ignoring the words of my Lord, who called our attention to "the weightier matters of the law, judgment, mercy, and faith . . ." (Matt. 23:23).

There are six major categories in which the average family spends its income. Around these six types of expenditures revolve practically all the activities of the human race.

The "necessities" come first, with *food* at the top of the list. Next we should probably list *clothing*. Of course, a person or family must decide on its own spending capacity for these needs, but everyone considers them as essentials when discussing budgetary planning. Members of the human family should also have *shelter*, protection from the elements. In a civilized society, they must either build, buy, or rent a place in which to live. The family home is a unit in most contemporary cultures, and a portion of the family income must go to provide housing.

Nearly one-half of American industry is engaged in providing for our need for food, clothing, and shelter. The fact that these basic necessities must be supplied does not license one's spending all available income and time meeting *only* these needs, if it is possible to do otherwise. Heads of households are worse than infidels if they do not provide for their own family, but they are fools if all their time, thought, income, and effort are used to provide nothing more than these essentials.

Next in line for consideration in the average family budget is *education* of the children. Schooling is not just an optional part of our national way of life; today education is "a must." Parents have not fulfilled their duty to their children until they have provided the best possible educational opportunities for them. A generous share of the family income should go for education and/or technical training. God has said, ". . . giving all diligence, add to your faith virtue; and to virtue knowledge" (2 Peter 1:5).

God's plan for his creative masterpiece—mankind—is an individual with a healthy body, an alert and well-trained mind, a good social adjustment, and a deep and sincere consecration to God. Exaggerated emphasis on any one area leads to maladjustment. The Lord himself developed all four aspects: "And Jesus increased in wisdom [mental development] and stature [physical growth], and in favour with God [spiritual life] and man [social skill]" (Luke 2:52).

The highest physical and mental development of any individual is possible only through a reasonable amount of *recreation*. It is not irreligious to spend one's free time enjoyably. Recreation means the act of re-creating. Leisure activities re-create an optimum energy level and stamina. To maintain your highest level of productivity you must frequently release yourself from the routines of life to relax your body and mind. That, too, may require a modest expenditure.

Finally, a part of each individual's income goes to support organized *government*. Taxes must be paid by citizens in exchange for the services provided by city, county, state, and national governments. Anyone who is loyal to his or her nation gladly pays a rightful proportion of the expenses of the governmental branches that protect and secure that person's general welfare. Since thoughtful men will certainly acknowledge that competent civil authorities are worthy of support, these expenses must be included in any plan of stewardship.

Boundaries of Christian Stewardship

God grants his greatest blessings to his children only when they walk in obedience to his will. We have learned that our faithful stewardship in all areas of life is an important part of his plan. If, then, we want God's blessings in our lives, we will be the kind of stewards he wants us to be. But what does that mean?

Where to Begin

God's church has the potential to bring both temporal and spiritual benefits to any individual, community, state, or nation. Nevertheless, multitudes of people never enjoy these blessings. They pass the church by, neither entering its doors, giving toward its support, nor speaking a word in its praise. Sad to say, even many self-proclaimed Christians never go to church unless there is a wedding or funeral to attend—or perhaps for Christmas and Easter services.

The church is like a great tree sending out massive, wide-spreading branches on which fruit ripens every day of the year. There are millions who come together under the shelter of that tree and who partake of its fruit. Yet many give never a thought to the tree itself, or the cost in time, money, labor, prayer, and spiritual struggle to those who have made the tree fruitful.

A good place to begin one's personal stewardship practices is at the house of God, the hub from which our praise and service radiates. There is never any question as to whether it is right or wrong to participate with the church of the Lord Jesus Christ in its efforts to minister to suffering people and proclaim the saving gospel to a world needing light, life, and hope.

Is There Any End?

Overwhelming blessings, overflowing happiness, benefits beyond computation—these are the promises of the Lord of heaven and earth to those who recognize his Lordship and acknowledge it in the way he has prescribed. To those who are faithful stewards he says he will "open you the windows of heaven, and pour you out a blessing, that there shall not be room enough to receive it" (Mal. 3:10).

Here is an abiding Old Testament promise, plain and positive, given to those who are faithful in their stewardship. This promise was made by the God of the harvest, the Ruler of the day, the night, the dew, the rain, the soil. He will provide all things in abundance. Is there any end to our responsibilities as his stewards? No—for there is no end to the goodness of God!

Love Is the Answer

It is often pointed out that there is a divine philosophy clearly evident in human history. A proper understanding of this philosophy discloses that the rise or fall of nations and individuals is ultimately dependent upon God and his will, not upon human might and power. The determining factor in a nation's establishment, growth, prosperity, and continuance or overthrow is its citizens' attitude toward God, their relationship to him, and their conformity to his purpose here on earth.

This is no more true, however, than the companion truth that there is a divine philosophy underlying individual human life. A person's success and prosperity, or impoverishment and failure, is dependent on God, not on human ability, sagacity, skill, or power. But let no man pledge his allegiance to God because of fear or to barter in the expectation of gain! Instead, out of a heart full of love, let each man yield his love and substance to the God who made him and wants only the best for him. Love should be the great motivating factor in the life of every faithful steward of the Creator's gifts.

3

A Christian's Value System

Immeasurable Assets

"Wealth" is usually thought of in terms of tangible possessions—the things to which a definite monetary exchange value can be assigned. There are a number of abstract values, however, that can be neither bought and sold in the public markets, nor allotted a price tag in the language of currency.

The "influence" of a good newspaper is an important intangible asset, for example. Yet circulation figures alone cannot fully reveal its influence. Similarly, neither does the quality of the paper used or the technology of the presses determine a publication's value. Even the style in which the news is dispensed cannot fully determine a newspaper's worth. "Influence" is an intangible value—the place the paper holds in the hearts of its readership. But it is a quality that must be considered part of the paper's total worth.

When a young doctor agrees to take over the practice of a beloved soon-to-retire physician, the newcomer receives many intangible assets. He benefits directly from the confidence of the people in the older doctor and indirectly through the trust the older doctor has shown in him. Respect, goodwill, friendliness, will be immeasurable values of great importance in his new practice.

Patents, copyrights, trademarks, and favorable locations are business values of an intangible nature. When an established business sells out to a new owner, all these—and even the name of the old company—may remain. If the public's opinion of the older company has been positive, reminders of the past are valuable to the new owner.

Faith and confidence are intangible assets. Faith in a government gives value to its money. Confidence in the banking system makes savings accounts and checkbook payments reasonable financial transactions.

The story is told of a bank whose customers began to lose confidence in its directors. At that time there were no insurance safeguards, and the depositors began to withdraw their money solely on the basis of rumored "troubles." Although the books were in order, and there was no cause for alarm, the breeze of an ill wind had reduced the confidence level of the public. Just as a great crowd of depositors had assembled in the small-town bank to make withdrawals, one of the largest depositors walked in and added a large sum of money to his account. One by one, depositors returned their already-withdrawn money. The bank was saved because the intangible value of confidence was restored.

Knowledge cannot always be expressed in terms of money, but it too has a tremendous value. For example, the technical knowledge of one man might make him worth $50,000 a year to a certain employer, while lack of that expertise would make him of little or no value in that position. (And the technical know-how would be worthless if the man aspired to lead an orchestra!)

Some time ago, a technician was called to repair a complicated machine. When he arrived, all he did was tap two or three times on one part of the apparatus. His bill for the job was $500.00. The enraged customer demanded an itemized statement, and the next day he got one. It read, "For tapping equipment, $1.00; For knowing where to tap, $499.00."

Did you ever think of "enthusiasm" as a quality of great value? This virtue, sometimes called "college spirit," is often a very important asset in business, in religious service, and even at home. It too, has an intangible value.

Names of well-known individuals are often connected with a business or a civic project for publicity purposes. Because of the value of their prestige, they are placed on the board of directors, or their names are printed on the letterhead of the firm or civic organization. Their names earn the public's confidence and appear to add stability to the project. An individual's reputation (whether deserved or not) is a vital factor in how he or she is seen by others.

Stewardship of Intangible Values

Christian people make up a great part of the intangible wealth of a nation and have the potential to make the largest contribution to society of any group of people. They usually add confidence, faith, integrity, and other high values to the civilization in which they live. A banker once remarked about a humble church elder, "I would hate to see that man leave town; he is worth at least a thousand dollars a year to this town, just by walking up and down our streets."

There is no doubt that God-fearing men and women are valuable to any community. A certain agnostic was planning to move his family into a town until he learned there was not one church in the community. He refused to move—on the basis that he would not want his children to grow up in a community where there were no religious influences!

The inevitable conclusion is that Christians must exercise proper stewardship over their intangible wealth just as diligently as they administer their financial assets. The kingdom of God cannot be established with money alone. Yes, we must be faithful stewards of money, but we must also nurture and protect the intangible qualities that help preserve the value of that money and the society producing it.

Stewardship of Personal Influence

Nature works its power in the realm of "atmosphere." The sun gushes forth light and heat; the delicate violet's aroma wafts beauty despite its tiny size; spices permeate the house with sweet odors; and an invisible magnetic field can lift tons of iron.

If we had tests precise enough, we would doubtless find that each man's personality is the center of measurable influences, all of which reach outward. If light is in him, he shines. If darkness rules, he shades everything around him. If his heart glows with love, he warms others. If his heart is frozen with selfishness, he chills them. If he is corrupt, he poisons all within his sphere of influence.

The sun in all its splendor and glory is not half so wonderful as the influences of a good person's life. If someone is a Christian, his or her influence must always be on the side of righteousness, whether it be in politics, commerce, or a social situation. When a moral question is involved, there is only one side on which a true Christian can stand, as the following story illustrates.

During one summer season, the vice-president of a Bible college spoke for nine consecutive weeks in several

A Christian's Value System

state-directed youth camps. His routine was to leave one camp after it closed on a Friday and arrive at another camp on Monday morning. Over the weekend he would be with his family and take care of mail and other official school business while his wife prepared his clothes for the following week of camp. One weekend this man was delayed in arriving home until late Saturday. His wife suggested that he take all his laundry to a local laundromat the next morning. He refused, on the basis that some student—young in years and young in the Lord—might see him and wonder why the official was doing laundry on Sunday and not visiting the house of God. The student would not have known that his mentor had been in church twice each day all week and that he had to start traveling to the next camp that very afternoon. All the student would have seen was an influential Christian who—like himself—was not in church on Sunday morning! <u>Mature Christians in positions of leadership have a special responsibility to set a good example for</u> babes in Christ.

Stewardship of Time

The average wage earner works eight hours a day, sleeps another eight, and has about eight extra hours in which he or she can find time to do many good things in a family or community setting to help forward the cause of Christ. It is as much a sin to waste time as it is to waste money. People can always find the time to do everything they really want to do. Since eternal values are at stake, and since God uses people to build his kingdom, he must have stewards who willingly put their time at his disposal.

Each week has 168 hours. Is it not logical to think in terms of a portion of this time being dedicated to God? Yet how many Christians tithe their time? For example, if 10 percent of the 168 hours were allotted to God's purposes, this would be sixteen hours and forty-eight minutes. Discounting the leftover minutes, this would leave sixteen hours. Then allocate them as follows each week:

Two hours of morning worship each Sunday

Two hours of worship on Sunday evening

Two hours for midweek prayer meeting

Two hours in the study of God's Word

Two hours in prayer and meditation

Two hours in visitation

Two hours in conferences, choir practice, youth work, or other church-related activities

Two hours for witnessing

This total of sixteen hours for God still leaves one hundred fifty-two hours per week for self. How the heart of any minister would rejoice to see this aspect of stewardship practiced by his congregation. More importantly, the heart of God would rejoice—and, in the final analysis, the individual so dedicated would be a faithful and joyous servant.

A noted evangelist spoke one morning in the chapel service of a Bible college. His subject was how we used time. He said that he had not realized how important each moment really was until one day when he came upon an auto accident just after it had happened. He rode to the hospital in an ambulance with one of the victims. Every few moments the critically injured man asked, "What time is it?" For him, time was slipping away. Time did run out for the man that day. He needed only a little more—but time was gone!

Time is something every man and woman has in equal measure. It is part of each individual's intangible wealth. Ask yourself if you are a faithful steward of time and if you dedicate its use generously so as to please God. "Walk in wisdom toward them that are without, redeeming the time" (Col. 4:5).

Stewardship of Habits

Habits, both good and bad, are formed by repetition. An act can be repeated often enough so that the muscles respond almost automatically. For example, in the case of an excellent typist, the keys are hit without consciously thinking about them individually. They have been touched so many times through practice that a neural pattern has been established whereby, when a certain nerve is stimulated, a specific muscle responds.

As previously mentioned, all people influence for good or for ill everyone with whom they are associated. Our good examples of right living and clean habits often win others to the Christian life. On the other hand, carelessness or neglect may turn others in the wrong direction, just as surely as it undermines our own good intentions. "I find then a law, that, when I would do good, evil is present with me" (Rom. 7:21).

All Christians everywhere must continue striving to develop good habits that will influence men for God. Paying tithes, giving offerings, praying, studying God's Word, witnessing, living uprightly, and responding to the will of God without hesitation are wholesome and essential habits for the Christian. The behavior patterns into which we allow ourselves to drift either honor or dishonor our Lord. A faithful steward for God takes careful heed of which direction his or her habits take.

Stewardship of Service

History has crowned self-sacrifice as one of the greatest virtues. All through the ages, selfishness has been like a flaming sword of destruction, consuming society, bringing waste and ruin. But often, dedicated service by a noble few has repaired these ravages and achieved many great victories for individuals and civilization as a whole. In a democracy, the state and its citizens are deeply indebted to the patriots who gave their lives to secure liberty for all. The church owes much to the company of martyrs whose blood has crimsoned many pages in the book of time.

We Christians know that if we want to have lasting influence in this world, we must follow Christ's advice in all things. One of his most important sayings was that those who tried to find or save their lives for themselves would lose them, and that those who lost their lives for his sake would really be finding them. Service to God is rendered through service to mankind. If we love the Lord, we are to feed his sheep (see John 21:15–17).

What makes a man or woman "great"? The best-remembered heroes of the human race have been those who rendered the greatest service to others, not those who amassed the largest fortunes. When young people are choosing vocations for their lives, the guiding principle and ruling motive should not be how much they can gather from life, but rather how much service they can contribute to the lives of others.

Stewardship of Attitude

By his attitude, a man may kill an idea or make it come alive. Attitude alone can fan the fires of hope or douse them with pessimism and despair. A critical attitude, even if well intentioned, may greatly hinder the growth of young Christians or antagonize unsaved people. James showed great insight when he wrote: "And the tongue is a fire, a world of iniquity. . . . the tongue can no man tame; it is an unruly evil, full of deadly poison. . . . Out of the same mouth proceedeth blessing and cursing. My brethren, these things ought not so to be" (James 3:6a, 8, 10). James knew that through our words we reveal much about how we think.

The Old Testament, too, had some words about attitude: "And thou shalt remember all the way which the LORD thy God led thee these forty years in the wilderness, to humble thee, and to prove thee, to know what was in thine heart, whether thou wouldest keep his commandments or no" (Deut. 8:2).

Because hopeful enthusiasm can energize and challenge a person into taking action—just as surely as a gloom-and-doom approach can be paralyzing—expectations are often self-fulfilling. For example, one pastor, his education director, and other members of the church staff decided one fall to launch an all-out campaign for enlisting a host of new members for the adult Sunday school. The layworkers were enthusiastic and hopeful that their joint efforts in visitations and phone calls during the upcoming weeks would boost attendance enough to exceed the old three-month record, which had stood for over ten years. There was one gloomy note, however. A certain Mrs. Johnson, notable mainly for her negative reaction to most suggestions, had muttered a few skeptical remarks during the meeting (though she was pretty much ignored, as she often was in such circumstances).

When the final day of reckoning arrived for the grand total to be counted and announced at the Christmas tree lighting ceremony, the record remained unshattered, though it was short by only a few members. Mrs. Johnson smiled, almost as if in triumph, and remarked to the director, "See, I told you we wouldn't make it."

To this the director replied, "And what did *you* do to help?"

"Oh, nothing," said Mrs. Johnson. "I knew all along we wouldn't make it—so why waste my time!"

Stewardship of Life

For a Christian, all of life must be considered in the light of stewardship. Jesus told us to "beware of covetousness, for a man's life consisteth not in the abundance of the things which he possesseth" (Luke 12:15). God did not redeem the world with money, diamonds, and pearls. He gave what was far more precious: his own Son. The most valuable possession in the world is life, and yet the value of even one life cannot be estimated in terms of money. William Carey gave a life of service to India. Morrison gave his life to China. David Livingstone gave the best of his life—in fact, all the mature years of his life—laboring in Africa. The words of the familiar hymn, "Take my life, and let it be/Consecrated, Lord, to thee" are quite sobering. Yet they have been a guiding principle for so many "wise and faithful stewards," past and present.

Christians do not use their lives any way they want to. They know that life comes only from God and is sustained by his power. Life is extended or terminated at the will of God. All life belongs to God. It is a sacred trust and therefore carries grave responsibilities. What man or woman does not stand in fear and awe at the realization that life—with all its varied opportunities and possibilities for success or failure—has been entrusted to him or her by God?

Two of his devoted disciples, James and John, once besought Jesus for special treatment. They wanted his promise that they would sit one on each side of him in his kingdom. These two "sons of Zebedee" had enjoyed his confidence on many occasions, and all along the Master seemed to have shown them preferences. There-

A Christian's Value System

fore, they mistakenly thought they had an advantage over others and the right to ask a special favor (see Mark 10:35–37).

In principle, this same mistake has been repeated many times. Yet, almost without exception, the mark of a generous and godly person is that of humility. Christian stewardship will bring into focus all of one's possessions and abilities, visible or invisible. As Jesus said, "And whosoever of you will be the chiefest, shall be servant of all" (Mark 10:44).

Stewardship of Prayer

There is a little motto that hangs on the wall in many Christian homes. It reads, "Prayer Changes Things." Prayer also changes people. Luther's prayer life had a greater influence on his starting the Reformation than did his hurling of an ink bottle at the devil. The words of James: "The effectual fervent prayer of a righteous man availeth much" (James 5:16b) underscore Paul's "Pray without ceasing" (1 Thess. 5:17). Jesus was a man of prayer. His disciples were taught to pray, and it was a stewardship prayer: "Thy kingdom come. Thy will be done in earth, as it is in heaven." A Christian can do a far better job in meeting life and its many problems and the unknown future, if he or she has practiced stewardship in and through a rich prayer life.

William Branwell often spent as many as four hours in a single session of prayer. Charles Simeon devoted the morning hours from four to eight to prayer, and John Wesley spent at least two hours daily in prayer. John Fletcher reportedly stained the walls of his room with the breath of his prayers. John Welch thought the day ill spent if he had not spent eight to ten hours in prayer. He kept a plaid blanket to wrap himself in when he arose at night to pray. Welch's wife would sometimes find him lying on the ground weeping for the three thousand souls for whom he believed he must answer to God. Let such men as these inspire us to be stewards of prayer!

Who Sets the Standard of Values?

Many believers have a sadly limited vision of the nature and scope of Christianity. They are often inclined to think of the church as being weak and isolated, having no vital connection with life's stern realities. Some carefully discriminate between "religious" and "secular" interests. In so doing, they tend to classify money and what it can buy as "secular" and "worldly," as if never to be mentioned in the same context as spiritual and eternal concerns. Many of us have come to look upon material possessions as the measuring rod for determining our day-to-day values and goals, believing that we can separate our lives into two unrelated pigeonholes.

In proud admiration of his accomplishments, an affluent rancher looks on rolling prairies, dotted with herds of cattle and encircled by miles of fencing—and he smiles with pride because of what he has acquired. Or a farmer strolls through fertile fields and valleys, looking forward to the coming harvest of corn, wheat, cotton, or rice. He is pleased, too, as he mentally calculates the value to "progress" (and to himself) of the vast tracts of timber beyond. The industrial geologist affixes a monetary value to the mountains of limestone, marble, and granite he takes pride in discovering. Meanwhile, the financially successful manufacturer visits the mills and factories that represent investments of billions of dollars and says, "I'm rich!" Or the financier clips bond coupons and imagines an endless tangle of railroads, their shining strands of steel rails stretching from coast to coast. He announces, "These are *mine*!"

A Christian's Value System

But what are all these possessions really worth? Take just a moment and look in on man's hoarded wealth. See him smelting ore, coining metals, printing bank notes, storing bonds in time-locked vaults, measuring each of these with a standard of values based solely on supply and demand. Greater demand and limited supply skyrockets these transitory values to new heights and dimensions. All this is part of our efforts to satisfy "the natural man."

Jesus was talking about this very matter when he insisted that no man could build a successful life out of an "abundance" of possessions (Luke 12:15). Life calls for a much more substantial foundation. No man has yet been clever enough to build a great God out of small gadgets, although many worship the great fallacy that a bulging wallet is one's best friend.

Frugality, thrift, prudence, and other budget-related virtues are all of the finest quality, but anyone who has nothing more than these principles, fine as they are, may still feel poverty-stricken and helpless in an hour of dire need. A man who has given all his strength to the task of amassing a fortune may sadly discover in a time of crisis that he has paid too high a price for it. Some of the most important words of Jesus are: "For what shall it profit a man, if he shall gain the whole world, and lose his own soul?" (Mark 8:36; cf. Matt. 16:26).

Perishable Items

Jesus emphasized the importance of the inner man by calling attention to the fact that it is what comes out of the heart that either glorifies or defiles. "A good man out of the good treasure of his heart bringeth forth that which is good; and an evil man out of the evil treasure of his heart . . . that which is evil: for of the abundance of the heart his mouth speaketh" (Luke 6:45). Our ability to draw a distinct line between the spiritually profitable and the spiritually destructive identifies a portion of maturity in our personalities.

One of the greatest needs in this day is a clear Christian philosophy concerning money. Whether the scale of operations is pennies or mega-millions, every gambler, tax-evader, take-over schemer, and extortionist is the product of a wrong attitude toward money. Economists say that money is no more than stored-up labor that is used as a medium of exchange. To come into possession of money without giving appropriate service in exchange destroys the dignity of life even if it does not technically violate the "Thou shalt not steal" commandment.

A groceryman stocks his shelves with materials needed by the householder. For taking the time to order, prepare, house, and assume the risk of damage or business failure, he is entitled to receive a margin of profit. A clever manipulation of inventory to distort market conditions, however, is an altogether different matter—whether dealing with canned goods or financial balance sheets.

The basic principle underlying so many of Jesus' parables involved adopting the eternal values upon which the kingdom of God was based: "Labour not for the meat which perisheth, but for that meat which endureth unto everlasting life . . ." (John 6:27). Inseparable from this idea is the doctrine of stewardship. Whatever we put on, whatever is on the outside, whatever is tangible—that which can be seen and felt—will pass away, but the workings of our hearts and minds are eternally binding.

Duty or Privilege?

It is indeed a blessed privilege to be in partnership with God and therefore helping to promote his kingdom here on earth. Any "expenditures" toward that end ordi-

A Christian's Value System

narily do not represent waste or reckless spending. Most of the money, time, influence, service, work, and effort a Christian contributes for and through the church is used for improving or building churches, schools, hospitals, and homes for orphans, or for extending the gospel to the ends of the earth. A large part of this expenditure—whether it represents tangible assets or time and labor—serves as a mighty bulwark for fortifying the church and a tool for advancing its benevolent efforts through the years.

The challenge for a Christian to be a steward for God, to share his values with others, should never be considered a burden or even a duty. It is never too difficult to do anything that we really enjoy doing. Once we accept placement in the kingdom of God as a privilege, joy in his service becomes part of our extra blessings. Then we receive a reward in the process of doing his works, and an extra reward for doing it gladly.

4

The Stewardship of Personal Capabilities

A Divine Recipe for a Happy Life

The Lord promised through Isaiah: "For ye shall go out with joy, and be led forth with peace . . ." (Isa. 55:12) and "Behold, my servants shall sing for joy of heart . . ." (65:14). But were not those words to apply to the "New Jerusalem," to the kingdom yet to come? How can we approach that level of joy and happiness in this life, transitory though it may be?

Happiness is a by-product of service, but if we aim at the happiness rather than the service, we are sure to miss the happiness. No one can say with any hope of succeeding, "Well, I am going to be happy because, from this day forward, I am going to do only the things that make me feel good, and I will avoid doing anything that doesn't put my interests first." That person is sure to find misery as his reward, or at least wonder what went wrong with his plan. He missed the following essential ingredients:

"J"—Jesus First with Everything

Before Christians can automatically give Christ top priority in the great decisions and activities in their lives, they must learn to place Christ first in the small, everyday matters. It seems almost incredible that people can trust God with the destiny of their souls but do not consider him in the routine aspects of daily living. Yet happiness is related to how consistently we give him first place in our home, social life, courtship, marriage, and vocation.

Peter and John learned to put Christ first as they went about spreading the gospel. When arrested, imprisoned, threatened, and forbidden to teach or preach in the name of Jesus, they answered the Jewish leaders before whom they were on trial, "Whether it be right in the sight of God to hearken unto you more than unto God, judge ye. For we cannot but speak the things which we have seen and heard" (Acts 4:19-20).

Peter and John wholeheartedly believed they were servants of Christ, that they had been sent by Christ to do his will. They knew they must dedicate their lives to the glory of God regardless of what the price might be. They did not question the cost or consequences, for Jesus was Lord; he was first. Someday they would stand before him to give an account of their lives. They had resolved that he would be first in everything *now*.

"O"—Others Are Second

In the hour of his conversion on the Damascus Road, Paul recognized that his life from then on was to be one of stewardship. He asked, "Lord, what wilt thou have me to do?" (Acts 9:6). In Paul we see a Christian soldier standing at attention, saluting his commanding officer and asking only to know his leader's will—a Christian steward asking only to know the will of the Master. Saul, the persecutor of Christians, died on the way to Damascus. From a roadside grave rose a new man to be known as Paul, the bondslave of Jesus. Paul was to acknowledge

The Stewardship of Personal Capabilities

without reservation that life is stewardship, and he consistently dedicated himself to knowing and doing the will of Christ.

One of the first lessons Paul learned was the importance of "others." This former persecutor, who had fervently made it so hard for others, now found that "others" were important: to instruct him, to care for him, to protect him, and—most of all—to love him and be loved in return. We must learn to place high value on the personal worth of each individual in God's universe. Hear that great cry of Moses expressing his concern for others: "Yet now, if thou wilt forgive their sin—; and if not, blot me, I pray thee, out of the book which thou hast written" (Exod. 32:32). Do you care that much for others? Jesus cared even more, and he gave his life to prove it.

"Y"—Yourself Last

Throughout the Book of Acts and in the New Testament Epistles, Paul maintains an exemplary life of concern for others. He was truly unselfish, considering his own needs last, if at all. Before the elders of Ephesus, Paul said, "[You know how] I kept back nothing that was profitable unto you, but have shewed you, and have taught you publickly, and from house to house, Testifying both to the Jews, and also to the Greeks, repentance toward God, and faith toward our Lord Jesus Christ" (Acts 20:20–21).

The prophet Agabus warned Paul that suffering and imprisonment awaited him in Jerusalem, but Paul took a firm stand and cheerfully rebuked those who wept at the thought of his dangerous future: "What mean ye to weep and to break mine heart? for I am ready not to be bound only, but to die at Jerusalem for the name of the Lord Jesus" (Acts 21:13).

Paul could so completely place himself last because of

his great example, Jesus of Nazareth. Is this not to be true of Christians everywhere? Let us strive to make Christ our example in everything, which includes placing others before ourselves.

Jesus first / Others second / Yourself last—that spells JOY!

Basic Rules for Service to God

Every properly functioning earthly organization has a set of rules and regulations, written or oral, to govern the activities of those associated with that organization. In addition, individuals have self-imposed rules they apply in their daily lives. In fact, how much a person accomplishes depends greatly on how well his or her schedule is "organized," how well those self-applied rules are followed.

The Bible reveals a divine philosophy for human life—a set of universal principles. This wise code of life is not just a set of "do's and don'ts," but it does have guidelines we can use. God's rules show primarily that service to him is tied to our relations with our fellowman and how we handle our circumstances. If we truly want to accomplish all we can for God, we will further the plan he has laid out before us.

Born with Possibilities

Every human born into this world is a bundle of potential accomplishments. God does not discriminate. He is not "for" or "against" anyone. He has set up the system of reproduction by which all living things come into the world. Humans may have light or dark skin or black, red, brown, or blond hair. The color of our eyes, the size of our body structure, the level of our intelligence—all these characteristics come through reproductive processes the nature of which only the Creator can fully explain.

The Stewardship of Personal Capabilities

But what happens during a person's life depends very much on what that individual does with the potential he or she has. A person with "normal" capacities can become either a valuable and responsible citizen or a maladjusted liability to all society.

As far as possible, each person has the God-ordained responsibility to develop his or her own potential. One person with the capacity to become a great statesman may never enter politics, study law, or even go to college. Another person may have the potential to become a great musician or singer, but may be swayed by the lure of easy money to disregard his or her own obvious talent for playing an instrument or singing the scale. Individuals determine what they will do with their "possibilities"—their abilities and opportunities. Circumstances may influence the course of events—financial distress may forestall the pursuit of private training, attending college, or undergoing any number of other experiences that would further the development of one's potential. But ultimately one must determine what to do (or not do) with those qualities that make us each a unique person in God's Master Plan.

Mostly Average. If a graph were made for the population of the United States (or any other country, for that matter), with the lowest degree of what is known as "intelligence" represented at one end and the highest at the other, we could plot the frequency of occurrence at each level along the line, using the scores of a standardized intelligence test as a measuring device. An interesting fact is that the "distribution curve" of the scores is bell-shaped. An overwhelming majority of people fall in the middle of the continuum, or the "average" range, while a much smaller number are represented at *either* end.

Use What You Have. So far as overall intelligence is concerned, most of us are "average," neither geniuses nor mentally handicapped. However, God has also endowed individuals with specialized abilities and talents that may or may not be related to general intelligence. Thus, someone who is super-smart in mathematical theorizing may be very limited in people-handling skills. God does not expect you to manage a giant business corporation if you are best suited to be a schoolteacher or social worker. But if you do have the capacity for executive responsibility and administration, you should not be satisfied to spend your life doing routine jobs, whether they be shining shoes, digging ditches, or working on an assembly line.

It is the divine will that each person engage in tasks best suited for his or her own special talents, and to develop that potential to its strongest possible level. Although God does require all his people to use what has been given to them, he never asks the impossible of anyone. The Lord needs men and women with great minds and great hearts and great energy levels—"great" simply because they are dedicated to doing his will.

Some of the mightiest dreams of the intellect only a heart full of God can realize! Spurred by the New World discoveries of Columbus, John Cabot mentally blazed an ocean path toward its northern regions. But it took well over a hundred years for the Pilgrim Fathers' burning hearts to broaden that image into reality and the beginnings of the land we love. Minds may bring "civilization," but hearts are what bring it to lasting greatness.

Erasmus represents a pure *mind* who saw evils in the church establishment, but the Reformation was not achieved by intellect nor scholarship alone. What this scholar could not do, Luther, the great *heart,* was able to bring to pass. The combination of both is the perfect will of God. Romans 12:1 is a call to dedication for all Christians: "I beseech you therefore, brethren, by the mercies

The Stewardship of Personal Capabilities

of God, that ye present your bodies a living sacrifice, holy, acceptable unto God, which is your reasonable service." We show our thankfulness for God's gifts by using them as he intended. This is the sum total of all that God can expect from anyone.

Knowledge Comes First

The Christian life begins with knowledge—the realization that one is a lost sinner, but that God brings the sinner to himself through the shed blood of his own Son. The sinner searching for salvation must first acknowledge those truths as personal forces in his or her life and that repentance will seal this New Covenant with God. After becoming a Christian, the spiritual newborn matures and learns about other things to do to remain a Christian.

In all his writings, Paul emphasized the basic need for knowledge. He told the Ephesians, ". . . be no more children, tossed to and fro, and carried about with every wind of doctrine . . ." (Eph. 4:14), and he told Titus that a bishop must be "Holding fast the faithful word as he hath been taught, that he may be able by sound doctrine both to exhort and to convince the gainsayers" (Titus 1:9). Knowledge helps to preserve us from error. Having a clear concept of our Christian duty constitutes a great protection from error.

What Do You Know? Do you know that as a Christian there is no intermediary between your soul and your savior? That he is your Lord? Do you know that Christ *in* you is your living power, *under* you he is your foundation, *around* you he is your wall of protection, *beside* you he is your faithful companion, *over* you he is your loving Master, and *before* you he is your soon-coming King?

For anyone who has knowledge of God's love and of his plan for salvation, it is natural to act upon that knowledge. Happiness is brought about by doing, not by wishful thinking. The words of the Master emphasize this principle: "If ye know these things, happy are ye if ye do them" (John 13:17).

Acting On What We Know. Most Christians know what they should do to live for God, but some fall short of living according to their knowledge because they have jumbled their priorities. And they often learn through sad experience how necessary it is to *do* as well as *know*.

Immediately after an individual's conversion, he or she is usually enraptured with the born-again experience and very enthusiastic about being a good steward. Babes in Christ are initially faithful in church attendance and in witnessing, consistent in tithing and even giving above the tithe, fervent in prayer and Bible study, and generous with their time and talents on behalf of others.

As time passes, however, converts may find that their childlike eagerness to follow God's leading becomes less of an imperative in their lives. The routines of daily schedules intercede, and the pressures within one's job situation or family drain off energy that should be devoted to the Lord's work. It is then that even the most mature Christian needs to be reminded of who is to come first in his or her life, and whose bidding is to be heeded above all others'.

Seeking Godly Influences

We don't need a degree in psychology to discover that faith begets faith, hatred begets hatred, love begets love, depression begets depression—and so on. Proverbs 15:1 tells us: "A soft answer turneth away wrath: but grievous words stir up anger." That illustrates the principle that whatever frame of mind an individual may have, he or she exerts a corresponding influence on someone else.

The church, with all its departments, has an overall potential for bringing out the best qualities in its congregation. The Sunday school influences through teaching God's Word. The choir helps spread the gospel of love through singing. Various missionary endeavors help men and women of God take the message of salvation to others and so change lives in a positive way. All these influences are vital to the work of God.

Recognizing the Power of Human Examples

As gentle as the atmosphere about us may seem, it actually weighs upon us with a pressure of fourteen pounds to the square inch. Even a tiny newborn infant does not feel its weight, and neither does the leaf of the aspen or the wing of a bird. But it is there, and no living thing could exist without it. Very much like this is the gentle, yet powerful and shaping, moral influence of a good man or woman. The world needs that godly influence, that "still small voice" (1 Kings 19:12).

As Others See You. "Reputation" plays a big role in every individual's life, which is sometimes unfortunate, since it is not always based on fact. Reputation is how other people see you—what they think you are like—and it does not necessarily reveal your real "self." A given person's reputation may be more or less make-believe, since it is not that difficult to convince most people that one is a very fine citizen, while the contrary may be closer to the truth.

As God Sees You. "Character" has a different meaning altogether from "reputation." Your character is the real you—what God sees when he looks into your heart and mind. Character, of course, is much more significant than reputation, which may camouflage, shade, and otherwise misrepresent an individual's qualities. Character shows who you are without your pretenses and disguises. In the long run, it is impossible to fake good character. It is true, it is real, it is solid, it is wonderful. God recognizes it—and so will your fellowman eventually!

Reacting to Opportunity

Since both your true character and the immediate circumstances determine how you react to the opportunities you meet in life, timing is all-important. The world of nature provides ample evidence that "To every thing there is a season, and a time to every purpose under the heaven" (Eccles. 3:1). In winter the soil resists the plow, the sun's heat is dissipated, and seed refuses to sprout. In spring comes the opportune time for all the forces that further growth. The sun generously lends warmth; the clouds send rain; the soil offers its fertility. Then must the sower go forth and sow, for nature has brought the opportunity that cries for a human response.

Some men have lost a fortune, a war, even their lives, because they did not respond when opportunity knocked. They were afraid to venture, to take a step by faith, to launch into the deep, to walk into uncertainty. So, too, do believers sometimes ignore or reject the invitation to wield their positive influence on society.

Opportunity to win others to Christ has knocked for many who, by failing to answer, are left with remorse of conscience to torment them forever. People often have in their grasp golden opportunities to practice stewardship and help promote the kingdom of God. Some have refused to respond because of selfish greed, and God's work has been hindered. God will hold us all responsible

The Stewardship of Personal Capabilities

for responding to the opportunities we have had to work for the Lord. How else is God to judge us—his children—if not by what we have or have not done with what he has given us.

Jesus taught his disciples how to pray, and that prayer is still a model for his disciples of today. He told them to say, "Our Father." The first-person-plural pronoun means that God is accessible to all people everywhere. Jesus did not say that only the poor could call God "Father," nor that only the rich could use that term. Regardless of either innate or circumstantial differences, he is Father—to the learned and illiterate; the black and white and yellow and red; those in the Social Register and in assistance programs. God can be called Father by *all* mankind.

There was a bit of urgency in Paul's letter to the church of Galatia when he wrote, "Bear ye one another's burdens.... *As we have therefore opportunity,* let us do good unto all men, especially unto them who are of the household of faith" (Gal. 6:2, 10, italics added). *Today* is the time to witness, the time to practice stewardship by giving of material goods, the time to pray, the time to teach, the time to work, the time to win, the time to advance the kingdom of God.

". . . behold, now is the accepted time; behold, now is the day of salvation" (2 Cor. 6:2; cf. Isa. 49:8). ". . . now it is high time to awake out of sleep: for now is our salvation nearer than when we believed. The night is far spent; the day is at hand . . . let us put on the armour of light" (Rom. 13:11–12).

5

The Christian Steward's Organizational Plan

Developing Teamwork

Since we human beings carefully and systematically "organize" as a strategy for success in every line of business, it seems altogether advisable to use the same principle for the most important venture in the world—the Lord's business. No believer is ever excused from participation in stewardship practices, so every person in the church should be taught to develop the qualities of a faithful steward.

Begin with the Children

As part of their stewardship, Christian parents owe their children "the best of everything," although it is the parents' right and responsibility to decide what really is "the best." Children are perhaps the most valuable asset of a Christian home. They are the most lucrative investments into which parents can put time, money, and effort. Everything parents can possibly add to the normal development of body, mind, heart, and soul should be provided for their growing children.

Children do not come into the world with ideals, attitudes, prejudices, and opinions. These are formed by observing the words and actions of those around them, starting at a very young age. A child's desire or lack of desire to be useful in the world, and in the church, will be determined by the early teaching and examples to which that child is exposed. If there are to be better home environments, better churches, better cities, better nations, and a better world, Christian parents must lay a godly foundation in the lives of their children. A major part of that base is Christian love.

Apply the Love Principle

There are values in life that far exceed food, clothing, and shelter. The most important of these values is God's overflowing love for mankind, his greatest creation. One of the purposes of Christ's mission to earth was to reveal the Father's universal love. Christ's example taught the children of weakness and misfortune to bear up under adversity, to sing songs in the darkest midnight, to march on to victory—and all because God loves them.

Love perfects. What health is to the body, what sweetness is to the lark's song, what perfume is to the rose, love is to personal character and to a society's value system. Disobeying the law of fire, man is burned; disobeying the law of steam, man is scalded; disobeying the law of love, man brings loneliness on himself and misery in varying degree to others.

He who loves scholarship will make haste to own books and use their wisdom for good purposes. He who loves friends will make himself available and "friendly." When aimed at the weak and the poor, love fulfills the law of self-denial. Our love for God is best expressed in a twofold desire: to worship him and to serve him. Love is part of fulfilling our obligation to the Lord. These things we must teach our children.

Just as individuals change their opinions, reactions,

interests, tastes, and desires with physical maturity, so do they change spiritually. A healthy and properly nourished child grows stronger with the passing years. A Christian nourished with love grows stronger in faith, service, sympathy, stability, and other manifestations of the fruits of the Spirit.

Use the Three "A's" of Application

Newly formed organizations usually enjoy at least one advantage: they have a very strong spirit of camaraderie in their ranks. The first-century church experienced this sense of fellowship and unified purpose. Since it seemed of prime importance to maintain this fellowship within the group, all the individuals held themselves responsible for each other's good name and peace of mind.

John Wesley established a group he called "class leaders." These leaders were to call on each member committed to their spiritual care. They were to inquire about spiritual health and need for material assistance and in every way possible bind them to the group. The resulting sense of unity was very strong, which may explain to some extent the early phenomenal growth of Methodism.

A profound respect for Christian fellowship and a corresponding concern for the spiritual nurture and growth of each individual will gain vitality for today's church, too. Anything that tends to weaken or destroy the spirit of unity among believers is a sin in the sight of God. Early in the lives of children, we must help them experience the three "A's" that underscore the fellowship and unity of the church. Then they will grow up feeling part of the organization and dedicated to its principles.

1. *Affection.* The writer of the Book of Romans set the emotional tone for Christians regarding their attitude toward one another: "Be kindly affectioned one to an-

other with brotherly love; in honour preferring one another" (Rom 12:10). No man loves God if he has no love for his fellowman. It is a command from God that we love one another, and this is the trademark of a Christian. Jesus Christ told us: "By this sign shall all men know that ye are my disciples, if ye have love one to another" (John 13:35).

2. *Acceptance.* One of the worst feelings a person can experience is that of being unwanted. Social approval or the lack of it is a powerful factor in human behavior. Nothing in the life of a youngster is so frustrating as an underlying feeling of insecurity, a belief that "I am not wanted in this house."

Juvenile delinquency in its varied forms can often be traced back to that sense of unacceptability, of not "belonging." Physical inconveniences and deprivations of all kinds cannot do nearly as much damage to a young person as not being accepted within his or her biological family. So, too, brick buildings, comfortable pews, and beautiful organ music will never take the place of the warmth that is meant to be found in the fellowship of a Christian body of believers—God's family.

3. *Approval.* A little encouragement sends a message of approval and has a much better influence on behavior than criticism. A nonbeliever taught me this lesson when I was only a lad. Our Sunday school was on a picnic one beautiful but hot day in July. There was a large barrel of lemonade for all to enjoy. As the people came by and filled their containers with lemonade, someone took a sip and complained that it was not sweet enough. An unconverted man who had been brought as a guest took a sip of his and said, "It sure is good and cold!" Then he added, "If you can't say anything good about it, don't say anything at all." He was right: the lemonade *was*

good and cold. And his attitude of approval made a positive impression on the rest of us. Negative comments foster defensiveness and are counterproductive.

Reaching Christian Adulthood

Ordinarily, our society for the most part thinks in terms of girls reaching physical maturity in their late teens and boys perhaps a few years later. (Of course, an individual may achieve physical maturity before or after the "average.") Emotional maturity may be reached about that same time, much later, or maybe never.

Certain characteristics identify the amount of progress an individual has made toward reaching emotional adulthood. A young child will say, "This is my dog, my house, my doll, my mamma, my ball." The words *I, me, my,* and *mine* are learned early. Children think in terms of themselves. No matter how inconvenient it may be for everyone else, babies and youngsters concentrate on being comfortable and happy, which means having what they want when they want it. If an individual reaches full physical growth, and retains this attitude, he or she is to be pitied. Unfortunately, this is even sometimes true of Christians.

The familiar prayer—"Help me, bless me, give me,"— is a sure sign of spiritual immaturity. When people "grow up" in their faith life, they see the many people who need help. Then their prayers ask God to help someone other than themselves.

Love Brings Understanding

Being able to understand what another is feeling is a result of wisdom, intelligence, learning, and personal experience. Of course, without having had the same experience, one is hardly able to fully understand the emotional distress of someone who has just lost a family member in death or is undergoing some other deep pain. Probably only those who have walked in the lonely shadows of the valley of death can really know the anguish of a sufferer's heart. But the "love one another" command that is found among believers will find one Christian ready to "be there" for another and thereby provide the warmth of his or her strengthening words and actions.

The stay-at-home brother in the story of the prodigal son did not know what it meant to be "lost" and a long distance from home with nothing to eat. He had never felt the despair of empty loneliness all about him. Even so, if he had understood the meaning of love, he would not have complained about the feast, the gifts, or the grand music of the joyful reception given the returning prodigal. If his heart had known the pangs of sorrow his father had felt when the wanderer returned, he would have cried, "My brother was dead, but he is alive; he was lost, but now he is found; let us rejoice!"

Some people punish themselves because they do not even understand themselves, although it is not likely that anyone will ever fully reach complete self-knowledge. *Why* we do *what* we do, and *when* and *how* we do it, sometimes remain a mystery, even long past physical adulthood. There are times when we do things we regret as long as we live. We may feel that if we could punish ourselves severely enough, we might in some way justify our actions and find peace. But there is One who cares so much and understands so completely that he can bring serenity to the most troubled heart. The psalmist knew where to turn for help: "Create in me a clean heart, O God; and renew a right spirit within me" (Ps. 51:10).

Accepting Responsibility

Jesus plainly taught the doctrine of personal responsibility, and today's world clearly needs a revival of that quality. As recorded in Matthew 25:31–46, Jesus announced that a day was coming when nations, individuals, and civilizations must be prepared to give an accounting for the way they had lived. Everyone will be there on that great day of judgment. The records will be correct. There will be no mistakes. Everyone will be required to give an account of the responsibility he or she accepted or rejected.

Much of the success of our nation came from the past work of today's senior citizens, some of whom faced hardship many of us will never know and can barely imagine. The scope of our personal responsibility includes the men and women in that age group who need help now. The younger generation is responsible before God to care for the needs of the older members of the church. Ask yourself what you could do to make the final years of someone's time on earth a little brighter.

Look, too, toward the other end of the age scale. Modern parents are (for the most part) scrupulously careful about the formal education of their children. But, strangely enough, the average child is allowed to grow up much too ignorant of the fine art of accepting "responsibility," a term that includes accountability for one's own behavior and duty toward others. This training, which can be one of the most rewarding lessons in life, is pitifully neglected in many Christian homes. Most parents will work their fingers to the bone to obtain material possessions for their children. Consequently, the children end up expecting all others, even the church, to do *for* them, instead of approaching each experience with the thought of helping to develop the kingdom of God here on earth. "What can God do for me?" must somehow be turned into "What can I do for God?"

Putting It All Together

To keep God's whole program working effectively, individuals on his team must organize their lives to fit that priority. The church, too, must build its projects accordingly. Prayer and careful planning will help every man and every church department use every opportunity to further God's work.

Christian education, missionary training, individual stewardship, benevolences, and world evangelism are all to be thought of as parts of a common whole. Success for an individual or for a congregation is not the result of spasmodic effort, no matter how enthusiastic each revival of interest may be. It is steady attention to carefully coordinated plans and methods that keeps the whole church working toward a common goal.

Analyze the Situation

Before any physician would dare prescribe a procedure of treatment for a patient, he or she would first diagnose or analyze the condition. What is the trouble and what caused it? How may the trouble be treated? What results may be expected? How long will it take to see improvement? The cost of an analysis should never be considered a waste of time or energy. This point is clearly brought out in the teachings of Jesus: "For which of you, intending to build a tower, sitteth not down first, and counteth the cost, whether he have sufficient to finish it?" (Luke 14:28). What are your goals? How may you reach them? And whom do you have to help you? All these are important questions.

The Christian Steward's Organizational Plan   73

Find Jobs for Everyone

Every job in the Lord's work is a ministry for the Lord. If any task is necessary to further the kingdom of God, it is the work of God. Anyone needed to fill a position in the church fills that position as unto the Lord. There is a job for everyone. Although not everyone can be a teacher, a minister, a superintendent, or any other singular officer, there are numerous other jobs to be done, all with an interlocking unity of purpose.

Lifeguards on Lake Michigan work in teams. When one goes into deep water to save a life, there is another waiting on shore, prepared to give first aid to keep the life going. Similarly, those of us in the church need to promote an extensive soul-saving campaign that is paired concurrently with a strong soul-keeping campaign.

Yes, there is a job for everyone, either in soul-saving or soul-keeping. There are offices to be filled, classes to be taught, music to be written, songs to be sung, but those who do not find a niche in any of these capacities can have just as effective a ministry in being a daily witness, in visitation work, or in any of a long list of other tasks that must be done. And—just as there is a job for everyone—there is somebody for every job.

Dividing Responsibility. The work of the Lord Jesus is so varied that no one person is suited to do all that must be done. When Jesus began the selection of his first followers, he chose men from various walks of life. In the modern church as well, selecting workers with only one type of background would limit the boundaries of their thinking and experience. But using a variety of people enables God's kingdom to become broader in its perspective.

It is virtually impossible for one man to save a generation or even a country, but *one man* can save his own life by accepting Jesus Christ as Savior. The life of that *one man* may be the life upon which God and his church will depend during some hour of crisis. *One man* can maintain a family altar in one home, his own. *One man* can give one-tenth of his income to God's work, giving Christ mastery over his income and possessions. *One man* can fill his responsibility in his church so well that the minister can rest easier in knowing the work will be done adequately. *One man* can give part of his time to the work of the Lord, and thereby allow someone else to do another work. *One man* doing his best for the Lord will encourage another *one man* to do his best. The work of God is done by multiplying the efforts of *one man* at a time.

The apostle Paul dealt with individuals as members of a group of believers: the church, or body of Christ. Most of Paul's letters that appear in the Bible were written to congregations in the new faith. The membership was made up of individuals with different occupations. They might be tentmakers, as were Aquila and Priscilla. They could be rulers of the synagogue, as was Crispus, or homeowners such as Justus or Jason. When it came to the church, however, Paul felt that they were brethren between whom no distinctions should be made, except for the interrelated responsibilities all must share in the kingdom of God.

Jesus clearly pointed out this division of responsibility when Peter inquired about the service expected of another disciple. "Jesus saith unto him, If I will that he tarry till I come, what is that to thee? follow thou me" (John 21:22). Each man and woman must do a fair share of the work.

Placing "The Best" Where Needed. One of the distinguishing marks of Christians who accept their discipleship seriously is the interest they show in the welfare of others. When Paul declared that he was "a debtor both to the Greeks, and to the Barbarians; both to the wise, and to the unwise" (Rom. 1:14), the way he used these terms showed that he meant every person everywhere. The love expressed in the gospel of salvation extended beyond the boundaries of his own group. Is not the true measure of Christian experience the love held for one's fellow man? It is a relatively easy matter to love those of your own household, and usually only a little trouble to love those of your own community. But the Christian doctrine of love extends our obligation. We are to love all people everywhere, which means that we will want to ensure that each of them receives "the best" we can offer.

A deep love for those to whom the church ministers will help Christians make sure that those people who need them will have the best teachers, the best equipment, the best rooms. For example, investigate almost any Sunday school and ask, "Where should the best teachers be placed?" You will often hear that the better teachers should be placed with the upper age levels. But where can more lives be changed—among the young or the old? Carlyle believed that when a man or woman is saved, a soul is rescued, and this is wonderful. But he went on to say that when a young child is saved, not only is a soul saved, but a lifetime is saved, too. Now who would you say is the most important? Who truly needs the best?

Financing the Church's Work

When any cause of the Lord's needs help, the need is usually not primarily for money, but for people. The church needs believers who have dedicated their hearts and their possessions to God's work. Individual stewardship certainly involves the proper handling of our family income, since giving is part of our personal responsibility to God and his church. In that way every believer has the opportunity to minister at home and abroad.

Avoid Haphazard Church Budgeting

Someone should ring the death knell for sloppy, hit-or-miss methods of church budget management. On too many occasions church leaders have been brought into disrepute by careless financial methods. Sometimes appeals for funds have been wrong as to timing, purpose, or motivation. Wise business executives carefully and systematically organize their company's financing. Why should the same principles not be applied to the Lord's business? No enlightened and conscientious Christian will be slothful in being a financial steward for God.

Just as an individual plans ahead by budgeting for food and shelter, clothing, savings, vacation allowance, and other family expenses, so can he or she plan before God to administer personal income as a faithful steward. Ideally, this stewardship will include a regular proportionate return to God. It will also allow for the flexibility to provide emergency contributions to meet unexpected church expenses and special offering opportunities. A personal benefit from regular giving is the knowledge of one's faithful service to God. The benefit from the church's standpoint is the opportunity to plan ahead with the confidence gained from having an assured income.

Hit-or-miss stewardship depends on emotions, the day's headlines, even the weather. It is guesswork that appeals to the type of steward who gives only if physically present when the offering is solicited. This type of financial management in the church pays the salary of the minister only *if* the money is in the treasury, or reimburses the evangelist *if* it does not rain the night an offering is to be received for him. Haphazard giving means that Christian education receives help only *if* someone comes by and asks for it, and a missionary is supported only *if* his story is touching enough. "Iffy" stewardship is improper handling of funds intended for God's work.

Consider Proportionate Giving

In recent times the idea of proportionate giving has been added to the principle of tithing, and this is a healthy attitude for an individual or church to form toward the work of the Lord. No one should attempt to restrict personal giving to one cause any more than he or she should attempt to live on one kind of food. We all need balance in our diet. And the church needs our balanced giving.

If the Sunday school is doing a work for God—and it is: by teaching God's Word, training new Christians to live for the Lord, adding strength to more mature Christians, and winning the lost to him—then the Sunday school is worthy of being considered for special gifts. So, too, are the youth department, camps and retreats, revivals, the women's circle, and the men's division. Anything that is done for the Lord in the right spirit and way is worthy of support by the church membership.

All these ministries of the church are important, and none are to be overlooked. Parishioners often will have special interests in a certain ministry and want to give added support to that activity. To do this is fine, so long as it does not mean neglecting other necessary responsibilities. There are ministries of Sunday school and to youth in every church. Radio and television ministries, missions, and Christian education can also be of vital importance. Benevolences are needed for orphanages, homes for the aged, and many other worthy recipients. Good stewards of God's kingdom will see that all opportunities for advancing that kingdom will be supported.

6

Implementing Church Stewardship

Systemizing Biblical Principles

The major doctrines of the Bible are taught and explained repeatedly; their importance is unquestioned. Water baptism, justification by faith, the infilling of the Holy Spirit, and the soon-return of Jesus are proclaimed with a regularity that usually reflects the interest level of a congregation. But the subject of stewardship seems to be mentioned infrequently and then not very thoroughly discussed. This neglect is a tragedy. Without faithful stewards the other doctrines that are contained within the message of salvation cannot go forth as the Lord intended.

Since the best and most impressive method for teaching stewardship is by example, all Sunday school teachers should be faithful administrators of the Lord's share. Just as they teach salvation because they have experienced salvation, and they teach baptism of the Holy Spirit because they have received that infilling, their teaching about stewardship must grow out of lives that show the blessings that stewardship brings.

Identify the Needs

In those last few moments before Jesus died on the cross, he whispered, "It is finished." He had fulfilled his commission, had done what his Father had sent him here to do. But the work of Christ's disciples has not yet been completed. There remains much to be done. In America alone there are great fields still untouched by the meaning of the gospel message. Thousands of orphan children need loving care, as do equal numbers of homeless adults. Aged disciples, who blazed the trail for truth and righteousness and paved a path for those who would follow, are deserving of our attention during the sunset of their lives. The physical and spiritual needs in foreign lands are staggering. There are yet millions of people who have never heard the name of Jesus. Many large cities, and even entire countries, are without one missionary to tell the gospel story. Every church member should be made aware of this impoverishment and pointed toward becoming a true steward by working at the unfinished tasks awaiting Christians.

Individual Responsibility. No chain is stronger than its weakest link. This can also be said about the church, for the church is made of individuals. Chapels and fellowship halls, pews and furniture, and carpeted rooms do not make the church. They only provide a general and comfortable meeting place for the individuals who gather for united worship. Believers are cautioned against forsaking the practice of assembling together. The church's strength is built on the fellowship of its saints. Each individual in the group has the potential to either add to or subtract from that strength, and the combined power of all individuals in the church makes a mighty force for God.

New-Member Training. Any growing church will be

Implementing Church Stewardship

receiving new members continually. Even before they become an official part of the church family, these persons should understand that being a Christian is both a privilege and a responsibility. This includes adopting the practice of Christian stewardship, because a faithful follower of Jesus will abide by *all* his teachings. New members should be taught to support the church with their three basic possessions: finance, time, and abilities. If they learn to give to the Lord in every respect, they will be a spiritual treasure to the church.

Missionary Education. Missions is one of the biggest responsibilities of the church. Although there are many methods, many people, and many organizations to propagate the gospel, anyone who is sharing the message of salvation in word or deed is doing missionary work. Every born-again Christian can and should be a missionary, a witness for the Lord.

If home missions is taught as enthusiastically as foreign missions, both will grow in equal measure. Several vital steps precede "official" missionary service, and church members should know the importance of each step. First, the worker must have an experience with the Lord; God must call him into service. Second, the worker must then be prepared and trained. Finally, he or she must be sent forth backed by the enthusiasm of those left physically behind. Every step is important, as is support for every step.

Maintaining Flexibility. One of the chief reasons some societies have not progressed is that they have thought, "What was good enough for grandpa is good enough for me." Therefore, wide-awake ministers, lay teachers, and church finance committees should be constantly on the lookout for new suggestions and methods that can help do a more effective job of administering the Lord's share in a changing world. The church must heed the stories of missionaries, the pleas for support of orphanages, retirement homes for senior citizens, and Christian higher education. Then it must highlight the duty and responsibility of each member to support these worthy causes—to be a missionary without leaving home!

Use the Calendar

Although no stewards of God should ever relax their efforts, there are certain seasons of the year when emphasis may be placed on specific phases of Christian work. Churches invariably note Thanksgiving, Christmas, Easter, and Back-to-School Day in the fall. Some have special days or months for emphasizing certain doctrines of the Bible. This provides an opportunity for sermons on these subjects that may include a call for renewed giving of either service or financial help.

Report Results Regularly. Members of the church who are giving time, talent, and money to see the Lord's work progress expect to receive status reports from time to time. This is not a matter of distrust; it is a legitimate business practice. If members are informed regularly as to what is being accomplished by them through others' hands they will probably want to strengthen their efforts in some areas. The minister and the finance committee are obligated to be frank about the church's total outlays and receipts—for if all are expected to continue giving, all should know where financial matters stand. (The work of the finance committee is particularly important and arduous in large churches.) The objective of all church finance is to effectively conduct for the Master a big business, worldwide in its scope.

Schedule Stewardship Teaching. With a little planning, the average church could do a lot to help its members become faithful stewards by using the Sunday school, the regular church services, the youth activities, and every other phase of church life for that purpose. If there is a continuous process of solid teaching of the entire Word of God, stewardship will be taught in all its fullness—because it is part of that Word.

Unify the Whole Program. One local church found to its great surprise that four departments, supposedly teaching the same basic topic, either in part or as a whole, did not know what the others were doing. Nor had they ever conferred together concerning their work. At a joint meeting midway through the program, there were minor contradictions, a sense of conflict, and frustrating discussions about purpose and results. No one could claim that this church had a unified approach to what was in theory a very worthwhile project.

To make sure his people had an identical objective in view, one pastor gathered his teachers together each week and—as their spiritual leader—taught them the lesson. This may not be practical in every case, nor in keeping with accepted practice, but unifying the whole program under some type of action plan is the best way to get things done.

Prepare for the Future

Since programs initiated without thorough planning usually lead to trouble eventually, planning ahead is definitely part of wisdom! If church leaders plan at least a year in advance, they can use the experiences of other churches as guides and will also have time to gather suggestions from all sources to help the planning go well.

Visualize and Vitalize. What percentage of its possibilities does the average church utilize? Although it is very difficult to examine a local church and accurately weigh its potential, God will help those who are willing to examine their possibilities and look for ways to advance the kingdom. When a new potential is made available, trust God to help you realize it. No plan will work without the Spirit, the Presence who is the vitalizing force behind all God's programs.

Clearly setting forth the objectives of a program will guide its initial planning. Then should come the outline of how these objectives are to be reached. Charts, maps, pictures, and sketches will help visualize how all steps lead to the desired goal, and the quickening of the Spirit will vitalize individual efforts and the overall plan.

But God does not anoint methods and plans. He anoints his people! The Spirit of the Lord comes not on machinery but on men and women. Neither stones, brick, wood, mortar, furniture, nor office equipment work salvation. It is the Spirit of God working through human instruments that accomplishes his purposes. The fellowship of believers is the supply pipe for the flowing of God's blessings. God's way of reaching all mankind is through his dedicated, consecrated followers. Men with a vision and women anointed with the Spirit can mold a generation given over to the glory of God.

Work the Plan. When Queen Victoria invited the great pianist Paderewski to play in her presence, she complimented him on his genius, for surely he had a rare natural gift. The world looked upon him as extremely talented, but Paderewski informed the queen that he had not always enjoyed this standing. There was a time when he was thought of as only a run-of-the-mill piano player. But Paderewski made up his mind that the world would someday call him a genius, so he went to work. He practiced for hours, he practiced for days. He practiced and practiced and practiced some more. Finally the world did credit him with being the genius he was, but only because he had worked to perfect the innate ability he already possessed.

"Plan your work, and work your plan" is an oft-quoted statement, but it is one cliché that bears repeating. Planning is necessary, but plans, however good, cannot work themselves.

Apply Godly Zeal. Imagine what would happen if every member of every church became zealous for the work of God. The congregation would thrill with a new spirit of life and power. An electrifying message would burn in the heart of every preacher. New songs would be written and sung to God's glory. The fires of evangelism would be rekindled in every believer's soul, and a missionary passion would stir the twentieth-century church. Because the need for trained, prepared, and more efficient workers would be clearly seen, Christian schools and colleges would receive ample support to do the work God expects them to do. Individuality would be downplayed in working for the cause. All this zeal would hasten the return of our Lord—or at least establish more fully his earthly kingdom!

Providing a Divine Pattern for the Church

The church of the living God has been commissioned to do a specific task. Fortunately, it need not depend on human wisdom and planning alone to accomplish its mission. It has an unfailing and infallible guide—the Word of God.

It is in the Bible that we find our standards of doctrine—the mold for shaping character and the rules for regulating the Christian's relation to the world and its people. Written within the Word of God are the basic principles on which the church is established. These principles will inspire and govern our activities as individuals and determine which practices the church may follow in performing its task of preaching the gospel to every nation, kindred, tongue, and people.

The Church as Custodian

The church body is made up of believers equal in rank and privilege. All are authorized to administer their own affairs under the leadership of Jesus Christ. These believers have declared their death unto sin and resurrection unto a new life. They accept God's Word and the revelation of his Son as the final authority (Heb. 1:1–2). Over and above these truths, there is no appeal.

One of the functions of a local church is to serve as custodian of funds entrusted to it by the members. Since these monies have been designated for a sacred cause, the administrators must prove themselves worthy custodians of such responsibility. Everyone concerned must strive to be the wisest steward possible.

Advance Preparation. Just as any church advertises, prays, plans, and looks forward to workers' training courses, revivals, and missionary conventions, so should they plan and prepare for increased efforts in stewardship practices. A thriving church is not the result of luck, but rather of the wise planning and working of devoted Christians. To succeed, everyone must carry a share of the burden. This is the price of all truly great achievements, whether they be financial or otherwise.

Personnel Selection. Since the raising of funds and their disbursement are two altogether different matters, the personnel for each responsibility may vary in their qualifications. Let it be understood that there is to be no difference in the quality of service rendered nor in the level of dedication to either task. Each office is part of the whole program and equally important.

All persons involved with raising money to meet the

church's expenses should meet people confidently, speak effectively, and possess a pleasing personality. Anyone charged with the responsibility of disbursing those funds needs some knowledge of bookkeeping, must be able to use figures accurately, and be acquainted with banking practices. Regardless of other qualifications, however, no one should be placed in a position of leadership unless he or she is practicing stewardship on the personal level.

Preparing the Budget

The steps in budget preparation will vary from one church to another, depending on denominational guidelines, size of the congregation, scope of outreach projects, type of community involved, and so on. The following general procedure is usually followed:

Estimate Income. First consider church income for the past two or three years as a base. Then list factors that might affect income in the coming year. Include items such as economic conditions and business forecasts, predicted cost-of-living trends, any new industry or other changes in the community that might affect local employment and thus income of the membership.

Consider, too, whether there might be changes in membership numbers or composition. Is the community growing or shrinking? Is the housing market changing? As ages within the congregation change over time, potential income may change accordingly.

Here also should the nature of the church program be evaluated and re-examined in light of benefits and costs. Have some programs become self-sustaining or even income-producing? Should some be eliminated or expanded?

Finally, list the estimated sources of income and the

amount expected from each, whether from regular weekly giving, general benevolences, special offerings, and so on.

Estimate Expenses. After discussion between members of the finance committee and pastoral and lay leaders, most outlay estimates will include the following:

1. *Ministries*—salaries for pastor(s), educational director, minister of music, youth director, secretary, janitor, nursery attendants (if not volunteers); include expense allowances where applicable.

2. *Building expenses*—debt retirement, utilities, insurance, repairs, depreciation, janitorial supplies, new equipment.

3. *Operating expenses*—office supplies, mailing, advertising, telephone.

4. *Benevolences*—designated (e.g., retired ministers, orphanages, missions, radio) and undesignated.

5. *Education and organizational expenses*—supplies and literature for Sunday school, Vacation Bible School, music groups, youth organizations, library; funds designated for support of colleges, district departments, national offices.

6. *Miscellaneous expenses*—flowers, athletics, special events and speakers.

7. *Contingency fund*—for emergencies.

In most local churches, the completed budget is presented to the congregation for discussion and final approval. Although church leaders are unable to control the flow of income (except by their persuasive abilities), they can and should control disbursements. Except for a real "emergency," no expenditure should be made unless provided for in the budget. The congregation may delegate authority to the board to make minor revisions in the budget, such as for utilities expenses that exceed the expected amount. But an extraordinary item such as buying unplanned-for equipment or property should be brought to the congregation for approval or disapproval. If it becomes apparent during the year that anticipated income will fall short of the amount needed, action should be taken immediately. Either the rate of giving must be increased or expenditures reduced.

Increasing Church Membership

Every born-again believer should become identified with a local church. The resulting sense of belonging will bring a new concept of Christian pride and responsibility. Ministers should offer periodic opportunities for church membership through transfer or reaffirmation of faith and urge new converts to join. Membership in a body of believers will strengthen fellowship, which often saves new converts from giving up completely when they become discouraged.

Longtime members of the church should do much to make a newcomer feel welcome. Their prayers, friendly good wishes, and well-phrased advice concerning an "overcoming" life can be a big help. Church membership offers a certain degree of protection from worldly concerns—just as a loving home offers security for a child.

Application for Membership

An application for membership—whether detailed or informal—should provide church leaders with valuable information about the applicant's needs and abilities. It might, for example, show how long the person has been saved and what types of Christian service would most interest him or her. Some churches conduct study classes for applicants, elaborating on how the church can help its members and how the members might serve the church in return. Such an approach heightens the feeling of unity and responsibility of a new member.

Fundamental Doctrines

Every parishioner, whether a longtime member or recent convert, should be acquainted with the basic doctrines of the church. False cults and worldly influences continually challenge every Christian. A thorough knowledge of sound doctrine is a strong weapon against these evil forces. Paul wrote to the church at Ephesus: "That we henceforth be no more children, tossed to and fro, and carried about with every wind of doctrine, by the sleight of men, and cunning craftiness whereby they lie in wait to deceive" (Eph. 4:14).

The early Christians "continued stedfastly in the apostles' doctrine and fellowship . . ." (Acts 2:42). Timothy was warned to guard against anything ". . . contrary to sound doctrine" (1 Tim. 1:10). Paul also wrote that a steward of God should be "holding fast the faithful word as he hath been taught, that he may be able by sound doctrine both to exhort and to convince the gainsayers" (Titus 1:9).

Individual churches have different methods of formally receiving members into their fellowship ranks. Whatever ceremony is used, the emphasis on personal responsibility in stewardship should be presented. A member represents Christ, the church universal, and the local congregation. All three should have a good representation.

7

Stewardship and the Tithe

The Logic of Christian Giving

Most parents try very hard to give their children the best education they can afford. That is a natural obligation whose worthiness is rarely questioned. But no parents have fully discharged their responsibility to their children until they have taught them something about the logic and motivation of giving.

Psychologists talk so much about inner conflicts, tensions, split personalities, phobias, and divided loyalties that we are sometimes tempted to think that human nature is incurably bad, hopelessly twisted. But the power of Christ in a person's life can change that nature and thereby resolve the problems and frustrations he or she faces—or at least make them easier to bear.

Part of the reason for this change is that in Christ we find a person greater than ourselves and a cause greater than any other. When we give wholeheartedly of ourselves to this great person and his cause, we turn our thoughts away from ourselves and toward others. No therapy is better than wholehearted dedication of one's life to God.

Giving ourselves to God by dedicating our time, talents, money, and possessions to him creates a sense of sharing in his divine program, a sense of belonging to that noble group of men and women who are followers of Christ. Spiritual and emotional unrest often disappear simply by giving one's entire being to God. It brings balance to a person's life, and this is the logic behind Christian giving.

Total Giving

Just how do you give yourself to God? There are countless ways. You give yourself to God when you offer some money in behalf of a cause he would approve. Money can represent your time, your work, a part of your life. On that basis, a gift of money is in essence giving part of yourself to God.

The same is true of using your abilities for God's causes. When you sing, teach, keep records, help clean the church, take care of children while parents are participating in some activity of the church—all these are gifts of different parts of your life. Since your natural assets were originally given *to* you by God as Creator, your "thank you" includes placing them in his service. This is true stewardship.

It is true, of course, that a person can appear to be donating any of the different gifts in his or her life to God, yet give them for self-serving reasons. Then no true stewardship occurs. But when you give because you love God—and want to show that love by helping others—that is the stewardship God requires.

No one can build a successful life out of an abundance of possessions (Luke 12:15). Personal fulfillment calls for a much broader foundation. Individuals set their own goals, determine the methods employed to reach those goals, and in the final analysis shape their own eternal

Stewardship and the Tithe 93

destinies. But every Christian knows that abundant possessions do not bring happiness.

So often the rich man is the "poorest" man of the community. His fortune may have cost him everything worthwhile—peace of mind, family happiness, health, friendships, and respect within the community. Part of Christian maturity is having the wisdom to discriminate between eternal values and perishable goods. And the truly successful person chooses the former.

Leaving All. A casual observer may wonder if it was really so hard for those fishermen to leave their nets to follow Christ. Did they actually have so much to lose? But remember that fishing was a respectable occupation in New Testament times. The Bible mentions that James and John were in their father's boat with "hired servants" (Mark 1:20). That makes us think that the family business was prosperous enough to hire extra hands. These men were also respected as Jews by other Jews. Therefore, following Christ *did* mean not only forsaking their livelihood and leaving family behind, but also suffering social stigma among their fellow Jews. Socio-economic pressures and religious prejudices made following Christ a serious business indeed. The early disciples did leave *all* for him.

Matthew, for example, made a decision calling for drastic change in his life when he left all to follow Christ and his wandering band. Matthew was not a small-time operator. As a publican he held a responsible administrative position with the Roman government. But so strongly was he affected by the personality of Jesus that he said "Yes!" and forsook all to be identified with him.

God's stewards forsake all to follow Christ, recognizing that all their possessions, talents, time—life itself—belong to God. Therefore one forsakes personal ownership and becomes God's administrator instead.

Is Planned Giving Legalistic?

A complaint sometimes raised against systematic giving is that it is legalistic and places man too strictly under letter-of-the-law restrictions. Because of this, some people hesitate to pledge themselves to regular giving and instead prefer to be more flexible in their monetary donations. However, the economy of the whole world is run on pledges and promises! If our country shut down the pledge system implied in the tax structure and international IOU's, America would go bankrupt overnight. Many businesses could not begin to operate without relying on credit—a pledge to pay. In reality very few individuals could carry on for long without it either.

Examine a few examples of "pledges" in everyday life. Homeowners, tenants, and business establishments promise regular payments to the gas company if the company will supply the gas. Or, if the electric company will send power into a building, the user promises to respond with the prescribed amount set forth by the company. Some people pledge to the finance company a monthly amount for the use of an automobile; to the bank or landlord a certain amount to own or live in a house; to an insurance company a premium for protection in case of loss, injury, or death; to the appliance company installment payments for a refrigerator, stove, or some other household appliance. Others use credit in the sporting-goods store for fishing or hunting equipment or a new boat and in a department store for clothing and even in some grocery stores for food. Yet some hesitate to pledge regular giving to the church! This is something most difficult to comprehend, for who is more deserving of our promises than the church?

What Stewardship Is—and Is Not

Those who have made a thorough study of the New Testament have discovered one truth repeated six times in the four Gospels. Jesus himself spoke the words: "For whosoever will save his life shall lose it: and whosoever will lose his life for my sake shall find it" (Matt. 16:25). That is the very essence of stewardship.

The Rich Young Ruler. When this man asked Jesus what he must do to inherit eternal life, he asked a good question, and he may have had a good motive for asking it. Read Mark 10:17–22 (or Matt. 19:16–22; Luke 18:18–23) and look at his approach. Was he a good steward?

1. He did have the right desire, and few would question that. He wanted life eternal.
2. He must have been in earnest because he "came running" to the Master.
3. One must admire his reverence: he knelt before the Lord.
4. He substantiated a background of good character and had been a faithful keeper of the law.
5. There was a sense of humility about him in that he volunteered to make a public confession.
6. He had addressed the Lord in what he thought was a most acceptable manner when he called him "Good Master."

However, this man had overlooked one important requirement for all those who would enter the kingdom of God. He was not ready to sell all he had and give it to the poor, so he "went away grieved."

Parable of the Tenants. In this parable, which Jesus gave to the chief priests and Pharisees (Matt. 21:33–46), he was speaking both to and about them. The meaning of the story was probably repeated frequently in congregations among the first-century church. In the story, the owner of the vineyard is God; the tenants represent the religious leaders among the Jews; the servants sent to collect the rent are the Old Testament prophets (many of whom were killed); the beloved son is Jesus, and the killing of the son signifies Christ's crucifixion.

What does this parable have to do with Christianity today? It shows God's attitude toward his "tenants," all who inhabit his earth. He wants them to be faithful and just stewards, and those who refuse to be righteous stewards will someday know the Lord's displeasure. With the abundant life offered by God, man can be either a good steward or an ungrateful despoiler. The world belongs to God; as his creatures we will be held accountable for our stewardship.

God's Audit. When Jesus made his last trip to Jerusalem, he found in the temple one of the most shameful scenes ever uncovered. Money-changers and tradesmen were satisfying their greed at the expense of those who truly wanted to worship God.

God knows all about the gifts that are offered to him in thanksgiving. For evil men to prey on these funds for private profit will lead to divine condemnation in the greatest degree. Gifts offered to God are sacred. Besides their tangible worth, they are one of the most delicate and intimate symbols in Christendom.

God knows exactly how much each worshiper could and should give to his cause. He sees all who have love in their hearts—those who sing, who meditate on his Word, who pray, who teach, who preach, who keep records. He also sees those who walk out of the church with the Lord's portion of their week's earnings still in their wallets. Withholding that share is the same as using God's money for private use, as gross a sin as any other form of embezzlement. It is a misappropriation of funds. God knows all about such disloyalty and will expect every Christian to give an accounting when the final audit takes place.

Giving—Grace in Action

When Joshua stood before a gathering of Israel's tribes and shouted, ". . . choose you this day whom ye will serve . . ." (Josh. 24:15), he was reiterating the fact that God has given each of us the power of choice, the power to decide for ourselves the kind of life we will lead. When that basic decision is made, the results of our specific choices are an inevitable part of what is sometimes called our "destiny."

We are exhorted in God's Word to "grow in grace" (2 Peter 3:18), to "Lay not up for yourselves treasures upon earth . . . But lay up for yourselves treasures in heaven . . ." (Matt. 7:19-20).

Precious Promises

Precious indeed are the promises of God, but all of them are conditional. They will work only as individuals allow them to work in their lives. Nowhere in God's Word can we find a record of his promising to bless a rebellious, selfish, and sinful generation. Even prayer is futile when the petitioner refuses to take a moral stand against something in his or her life that is a barrier to receiving God's blessings.

Most of us would agree that there is something hypocritical about praying for a cause for which the person praying does not give full support—praying for the Sunday school class but refusing to teach a class; praying for the preacher but skipping church services; praying for orphans but withholding love from one's own child; praying for missions but being unwilling to go across the street to witness or reluctant to support a college that prepares missionaries for service.

The promise in Malachi 3:10 is that God will open "the windows of heaven, and pour you out a blessing," for which there will not be room enough to receive, but only after "all the tithes" are brought into God's house. Jesus told us that "good measure, pressed down, shaken together, and running over" shall come to the giver (Luke 6:38). According to the Book of Proverbs, "The liberal soul shall be made fat: and he that watereth shall be watered also himself" (11:25), and "Honour the LORD with thy substance, and with the firstfruits of all thine increase: So shall thy barns be filled with plenty, and thy presses shall burst out with new wine" (3:9–10).

Promises to Believers. Perhaps the greatest Christian who ever lived was the apostle Paul. He spoke for himself and on behalf of all believers when he said that "we were allowed of God to be put in trust with the gospel . . ." (1 Thess. 2:4).

There were three good reasons that God could trust Paul with the custody of the gospel. First, the apostle had heard and heeded a call to be saved from his sins and to be a witness for Jesus Christ. Paul's next call was the invitation to "come over and help us." The third call to which he responded was from within, to which he quickly replied, "I am debtor."

Today, God can still entrust the custody of the gospel to Christians who, like Paul, have heard and heeded the call of God. His promises are to those who believe his message of salvation. God extends his mercy, goodness, love, and blessings to those who believe and are thereby enabled to receive his eternal gifts. The highest love of which man has any knowledge has been revealed in Christ Jesus. His perfect love guarantees that his mercy, his goodness, his promises—all his blessings—are available to those who believe on him.

Promises to Obedient Followers. The selfish and disobedient characters in the Bible bear sufficient warning to those who claim to be followers of Christ that obedience is better than any sacrifice. Balaam confessed that he had sinned but continued in disobedience; Achan knew he had sinned but he, too, continued in disobedience. King Saul was aware of his gravest sin but continued to disobey God's commands. Double-minded Balaam desired the forbidden rewards of a heathen king. Though remorseful, Achan coveted forbidden treasures. Insincere Saul coveted the choicest of the flocks that the Lord had ordered him to destroy.

A famous child specialist once observed that seriously ill children recovered much faster if they had been taught to obey. The specialist estimated the chance for recovery of an obedient child to be four times greater than the recovery rate for a spoiled and undisciplined child. Let the children of God remind themselves over and over again of the great promises of God that are accessible to his obedient and faithful followers.

Binding Principles

A steward is not an owner. A steward is an administrator of someone else's property, an executor of an estate held in trust for another. A steward must dispense or put to use all he holds in trust according to the will of the owner and in such a way as to bring the owner the greatest returns. God places in the hands of his stewards the sum total of life itself—their abilities, energy, time, money, opportunities—and expects these things to be used to spread the gospel of Christ. On this principle must every true and obedient believer base all of his or her stewardship activities.

New Testament References To Tithing. Within God's program of stewardship, tithing plays a large and vital part. Both individuals and the church benefit from a regular and specified giving routine. The tithers benefit because the act of giving is a pleasurable experience that also delights God. And the regularity establishes good habits of giving that become automatic. The church benefits because it can project its plans with an assurance that there will be income to meet the needs of those plans.

God has not left us with any uncertainty as to the amount that we should allocate for his purposes. He has taken particular care to designate the exact proportion of each person's substance that this should be. He does not leave this to an individual's generosity or parsimony, to the goodwill or covetousness of those who benefit by the labor of all God's servants. The Lord does not consider this all-important matter as an optional choice for his followers. To have done so—to have left to the whim of believers whether his special servants would be sustained or left to suffer—would have placed his work in jeopardy of curtailment and defeat.

God has carefully established a system by which the maintenance and needs of all those who further his work of salvation are to be met and supplied. This act is characteristic of God. Throughout his entire creation, all things are arranged in complete harmony, and his laws cover every contingency. God cares for the needs of all mankind, so it would have been amazing had he not made provision for meeting the necessities of his church and those whom he has called to do his work.

The system that God has ordained for the mainte-

Stewardship and the Tithe 101

nance and support of those who are the heralds of his salvation is tithing. There are only six direct references to tithing made in the New Testament, but this is enough. Why should there be more? If God's Word only *once* declared it to be a requirement, that should be sufficient basis for practicing the system of tithing.

1. *Matthew 23:23.* "Woe unto you, scribes and Pharisees, hypocrites! For ye pay tithe of mint and anise and cummin, and have omitted the weightier matters of the law, judgment, mercy, and faith: these ought ye to have done, and not to leave the other undone."

This is from an address of Jesus in which he was pronouncing condemnation on the Jewish leaders' hypocrisy. He incidentally mentioned tithing, but that was not the theme of his address. It has often been pointed out that the only thing for which Jesus ever commended the scribes and Pharisees was their observance of the tithing law. The words ". . . these ought ye to have done . . ." leave no doubt that Jesus endorsed the principle of tithing.

2. *Luke 11:42.* This reference is almost identical to the quotation from Matthew. The content and meaning are the same.

3. *Luke 18:12.* "I [a Pharisee] fast twice in the week, I give tithes of all that I get." The Pharisee speaking here stood in prayer and thanked God that he was "not as other men" (v. 11). In this parable Jesus condemned this self-righteous Pharisee (and all like him). Being a Jew, the Pharisee was expected to give tithes of all that he acquired and thus should not be commending himself to God for doing so. This parable, however, in no way removes the tithing ordinance.

4. *1 Corinthians 9:13–14.* "Do ye not know that they which minister about holy things live of the things of the temple? and they which wait at the altar are partakers

with the altar? Even so hath the LORD ordained that they which preach the gospel should live of the gospel."

Although tithing is not specifically mentioned here, there is a reference to the Old Testament (Num. 18:21–24), where account is made of how the priests (which were of the tribe of Levi) were to be supported by the tithes of the other eleven tribes. The Levites were to have no part of the land except in the suburbs of the cities in which they dwelt and were to have no inheritance in the land of promise. But they were to be supported by the tithes of the other children of Israel. Similarly, says the apostle Paul: "Even so hath the Lord ordained that they which preach the gospel should live of the gospel." Here the teaching is very plain that those who are distinctly set aside as workers for the Lord shall be supported by the gifts of others.

5. *Hebrews 7:1–10.* This is a discussion of how Abraham paid tithes to the priest Melchisedec during the patriarchal dispensation. It also restates the tithing principle as it applied to the tribe of Levi. The writer then discusses the enlarged ideals of Christ's priesthood (vv. 11–19). He says of Jesus: "Thou art a priest for ever after the order of Melchisedec" (v. 17; cf. Ps. 110:4).

6. *Hebrews 7:20–25.* These verses continue the discussion regarding the Levitical priesthood and only indirectly refer to tithing. The words "By so much was Jesus made a surety of a better testament" (v. 22) imply that tithing is not because of law or regulation, but because of the new covenant of love established by Jesus on behalf of the work of God's kingdom.

Tithing Makes a Difference. Tithing is vital to Christianity. To be a Christian is to put God first in everything. To be a tither is one way to honor God's priority and accept our role as his steward. A man need not consider whether he can afford to pay a tithe but whether,

Stewardship and the Tithe

being a Christian, he can afford *not* to put God first in his life. The tither believes that:

1. God owns all things, and every Christian is charged with the responsibility of managing them for God.
2. A Christian lives under an obligation each day to seek first the kingdom of God and his righteousness.
3. A Christian has a right to depend on the love and provision of God under every condition.
4. There is a sanctity about all possessions because they are the property of God.
5. God honors the tithe when it is dedicated to him in a spirit of humility.
6. Tithing confirms the covenant between God and his followers. It is a mutually profitable and gratifying agreement between God and man. They become partners in the greatest of all life's busy transactions.

Offering the Remainder. Of course, after a Christian has deducted the tithe, which is what rightfully belongs to the Lord, he or she is free to give any portion of the remaining nine-tenths as an offering to him as well. When such money is deposited in the collection plate at church, it is an act of placing oneself at the disposal of God. Everyone cannot go to the ends of the earth to preach the gospel, but we can all send ourselves in the form of our tangible assets. Money in the collection plate or spent directly on behalf of those in need represents service the donor wishes to contribute to furthering the kingdom of God.

Stewards in the Home

Although some parents have an abundance of worldly riches, the vast majority of families seldom manage large sums of money. In the average home, the available funds must somehow be adequate for the many categories of expenses and obligations. How to stretch income over outgo is an ever-present conundrum, but there are two related questions to be considered: How does a parent teach children to use money and not let it use them? How best will a child learn about the claims of Christian stewardship?

Children need to learn (1) that all they are as individuals, and all they possess and acquire, belongs to God and (2) that they are his stewards. Youngsters learn about money by having money in their possession and discovering what it can do for them and to them. Good stewardship practices are learned by practicing stewardship, just as they learn how to balance themselves on a bicycle through the repeated experience of riding one or how to swim by getting into the water.

The Woman's Role in Family Stewardship

Civilization still revolves around the home and family—both of which may be said to revolve around the woman. Since a woman can either make or break the happiness in a home, it is a grave error for a man not to allow his wife to share in administering the family finances.

Money transactions relating to the home are varied and many. Whether or not a wife has an outside job, she probably knows more about the family budget than her husband does. Household needs are recurrent and often urgent, and they cannot be met without money. The wife and mother, by her very position in the home, is a money-spender. Some department-store owners estimate that 90 percent of all buying in their stores is done by women, their principal customers. Economists have estimated that 50 to 75 percent of the average family income is spent by the woman.

Though less common today than in earlier times, most people regard men as the principal breadwinners. In any event, wage earners may spend eight hours a day on the job. The sixteen hours spent away from the job keep one "in trim." By sharing the responsibilities of stewardship, spouses can help each other develop in their chosen vocations and consequently increase the family earning power. Women are in no way excused from this duty.

Unpaid Wages

The phrase "just a housewife" is very misleading! Any woman who sees that the children are off to school and home again, chauffeured by her to the dentist or barber shop, and properly clothed and fed has an important job. She also relieves the man of the house of a thousand cares and anxieties by ministering to the physical needs and morale of the family. A wife is thereby making a very definite contribution to the earnings of the family, even if she has no paid employment.

Stewards in the Home

As far back as 1923, the National Bureau of Economic Research estimated the economic worth of housewives to be over eighteen billion dollars. Allowing for inflation and population increase, this figure would certainly rise to a truly staggering amount today. But many women (estimated currently at one-third of all married women) are now by choice or necessity working outside the home to supplement family income.

Women have always made a significant contribution to the progress and uplift of the human race. On the *Mayflower* was not only a host of "Pilgrim fathers," but a sterling group of mothers who braved the seas, the dangers, the hardships, and eventually the toil of living in a strange land. Along with other women who landed on these shores, they became the matriarchs of that sturdy band of citizens who later wrote the Declaration of Independence and forged a new nation.

When the pioneer men developed the West, alongside of them were the mothers who taught their children by the fireside before there was an organized educational system. Just as women are still sharing in the development of the world and its citizens today, they have an important place in a family's stewardship practices.

Teachers of Stewardship

Let us be realistic and face the statistics—more women than men take an active role as church members today. For example, women teachers of Sunday school far exceed men teachers in number. Women also hold places of leadership in other organizations of the church. They have both opportunity and obligation to teach and exemplify the principles of stewardship. In fact, it is impossible for anyone to declare "all the counsel of God" (Acts 20:27) without placing proper emphasis on the fact that all people everywhere will eventually give an accounting to God of his or her service.

Most women Sunday-school leaders probably teach the lower age groups and thus have the enviable position of starting their pupils off with the principles of stewardship. Whether young children have a good understanding of the concept greatly depends on the instructions they receive at home and from their first teachers. Good stewardship—like other fundamental Christian doctrines—is best learned early in life.

Christian Parenting

In the writings of both the New Testament and the Old, instructions on the care of children are frequently given. God holds parents responsible for doing everything possible to influence their children toward righteous living. That we should "train up a child in the way he should go" (Prov. 22:6) is a sobering command.

A child's ideals, attitude toward money and other possessions, desire to be useful in the world—his or her whole outlook on life and the world—will be determined by the early teaching and environment found at home. Christian parents plant in the lives of their children the seeds for a better world.

Educating for Sound Values

Universal education is perhaps the most widely accepted obligation in our society. America seems to have almost always supported this idea since its earliest days. In the preamble of an act of our Continental Congress in 1787, our government emphasized (in referring to the Northwest Territory) that religion, morality, and knowledge were necessary to good government. Recognizing that a sound value system is necessary for the happiness of mankind, our first leaders insisted that schools and education should forever be encouraged. That trend continues today.

Not only is there a national need to make all citizens wise, influential in the world, and reasonably secure, there is also a need to make them morally strong. Even the secular educational system can do much to establish and nurture the universal ideals of liberty, justice, and righteousness. More than one political leader in the United States has expressed the opinion that Christianity is the greatest factor in civilizing, molding, and upgrading people of all ages. James Hill, a great railroad builder, once said it was a mistake to train young people in all branches of knowledge and give them the full college program to supposedly equip them for life, without making sure they knew and accepted the fundamental difference between right and wrong.

Any school system would do well to keep the Bible as part of its regular references. An educated conscience is essential for dealing with the forces and motives one faces when managing the big tasks in life. Only those acquainted with the Word of God can fully experience and appreciate the finest aspect of a full education: learning about the Creator's world. Unfortunately, outspoken proponents of "church state separation" have managed to have removed from the public schools almost all traces of the Bible, prayer, and moral instruction.

Educating for Christian Leadership

Christian men and women belong to one body—the church. Believing that this fellowship of believers is an essential part of Christianity, they are interested in the future development of the church. If they do not desire the church to lose ground, Christian parents would do well to train their children to dedicate themselves to some aspect of Christian service. When broadly defined, Christian service might include the work of home and foreign missions, teaching in a Christian college, being a social worker, or undertaking some other form of full-time activity that openly or indirectly furthers God's kingdom.

The Lord's work should be presented by those who strive to be the best qualified persons possible. The keenest and brightest young minds should be encouraged to enter the field of Christian service. The more capable Christian workers are, the more rewarding the results will be.

In the training of distinctive Christian leaders, Bible-based colleges are a necessity. It has been estimated that approximately 80 percent of missionaries, ministers, and other professional church workers have been trained in Christian colleges, with the remainder trained in state or private secular schools. Since every church college must have financial assistance to carry on its ministry of training God's modern disciples, Christians everywhere are expected to give some of their money to help endow and maintain these schools. If they do not do so, future Christian leadership may be weakened or even fail in its mission.

Family Expenditures and Christian Stewardship

Of perhaps equal menace to real spirituality and the program of the church are the world-oriented rich and the financially careless poor. Members with wealth often pay a large share of the bills but do not participate in the devotional or evangelistic work of the local church. On

Stewards in the Home

the other hand, those who mismanage family income sometimes take an active part in church activities but fail to assume a fair share of the church's financial burden. Stewardship requires both monetary support and personal participation. Its practices are not required of one group of people and excused for others.

Most financially secure men and women who attend church are open-minded and receptive to the concepts behind outreach and benevolences. They are usually willing and eager to listen to loyal preaching when it is done in the power of the Holy Spirit. Poorer parishioners especially want to be part of the church program. Neither liberality of spending nor limited means exempts an individual from giving heart and mind to the church of Jesus Christ through generous donations of time and service.

Children and the Family Budget

The family budget is not a mysterious, difficult-to-understand puzzle that must be kept secret from some members of the family. Facts about income and how it is to be spent should be discussed within the family, and each member should be responsible for an appropriate share of the decision making. Christian parents are not making a mistake when they allow their children to become acquainted with the family's financial affairs early in life, so long as the knowledge includes being taught how to face responsibilities. If children know the facts, they may be more considerate when making their requests for spending money or allowances.

One man reported to me that his whole family usually considered the household budget together, deciding how money was to be allocated. One problem for which they found a very satisfactory solution was the purchase of a new suit for Dad, who needed to be well dressed to carry on his particular line of work. The children agreed that (if necessary) they would be willing to take an allowance cut for a certain period, just so the father could be suitably dressed to maintain the family income!

In these days of widespread affluence, bulging savings accounts, full employment, and two-income families, the twentieth-century boy and girl have more money to spend on luxuries, pleasures, and nonessentials than the children of any previous generation. Large fortunes in business, bonds, and real estate are being left to mere children, and young people in general have never been tempted with so much wealth as they are today.

Some time ago, a certain Midwestern farmer died after working for many years to accumulate a 2,000-acre farm. He left the farm and his bank accounts to his two sons, who had none of the moral fiber their father possessed. It took the two boys only months to dissipate a fortune that the father needed a lifetime to accumulate. The farm was eventually sold for nonpayment of taxes.

Another man, a baker, worked hard and saved carefully. He left almost a half-million dollars to an only son who was, at best, lazy, but at his worst was nothing short of a renegade. He, too, squandered his inheritance in months. Raising children without a Christian concept of money places them at a great disadvantage, a position that can result in tragic financial ruin.

Was the prodigal son totally at fault? We may be overlooking part of the real tragedy in the downward career of the prodigal son. One cannot read this parable without seeing the words, "Give me the portion of goods . . ." and realizing that the father "divided unto them his living." The younger son, the story goes, wasted his substance with a riotous way of living and spent everything he had. Perhaps this boy had never been taught to take care of money!

Many sermons denounce the boy (and/or his unforgiving brother). But suppose the dad had not taught his wastrel son the value of money or rather its proper use. What reward is there for *any* father to make a fortune and then give it to a son whose use of it will mean his downfall? The money will be wasted, and the boy ruined and ostracized by many—even if his father does forgive him and celebrate his return.

Children and Stewardship

All Christians can and should teach their children the principles of stewardship. The best method of teaching is by one's own example. Parents can also include their children in the family council when they are old enough and talk over with them how the family can best administer their share of the Lord's gifts.

It is not fair to anyone, child or adult, if it seems that the father does all the giving. Each child should see that both Mom and Dad share as stewards. Early in life, children should be told that they, too, must form the habit of giving regularly. He who is taught to be "faithful over a few things" will learn to be faithful over much and will be made "ruler over many things" (Matt. 25:21). Children who see their parents giving to God will remember to do the same when they begin to earn their own money, especially if they have through childhood allocated a tithe for the church from their allowance. Any Christian who reaches the decision to give 10 percent or more of his income to the work of God has made a new confession of the Lordship of Jesus Christ, who is henceforth looked upon with more respect, love, honor, and worship. On the other hand, he who gives little—but could give more—learns to love little.

Family Administration of the Lord's Share

The Christian church bears a very intimate relationship to the Christian home. A home is not Christian if it exists separate and apart from the teachings of God's Word.

Many of the problems that arise in a home involve money management. One of the most common causes of dissension is the question of how the family funds are to be managed. Each half of a couple needs to come to a clear understanding of what regular bills are to be expected, whose duty it shall be to attend to them, and how their "personal" bills are to fit into the family budget.

When a minister can help a pair of newlyweds view all their income and possessions as a trust from God over which they are stewards (and thus responsible to God for administering those assets for the advancement of his kingdom on earth, including their own care and comfort), that minister has removed one of the greatest hindrances to achieving a happy home. If all possessions are viewed as a sacred trust, neither of the two will be inclined to speak of "my money" and "my rights." There is something unifying in the act of two people sitting down together to figure out their accounts and determining God's share of the profits.

Building Responsible Parenthood

Parents cannot choose to transfer their responsibility to a grandparent, a baby-sitter, a teacher, a friend, or even to the minister and the church. Children begin forming their characters as they watch their parents, who are their first and most influential teachers. A mother and father must assume the responsibility of guiding this development.

Nearly every Mom needs the assistance of Dad in the matter of discipline, but it is unwise and unfair to assign all discipline to *one* parent. Whether it is one or both parents who hold jobs outside the home, homecoming should be a time of joyful family sharing, not an occasion for judgment and assigning punishment. Busy parents need to put as much thought and initiative into holding their children lovingly as they do into holding a job or running a business.

Preventing Home Failures

Someone once compiled a list of the warning signs of "home failures." Among the items were parental misunderstanding of the child, excessive faultfinding, failure to express affection, lack of trust and confidence between parents and children, drunken parents, separation or divorce, loss of a parent by death. Three parental statements can mean more to a child than having an array of possessions piled at his feet: "I love you. I appreciate you. I am proud of you."

Although many parents do not take the time to understand the viewpoint of their children, each mom and dad should aim at staying young enough at heart to keep in sympathy with their growing boys and girls, who all too soon will be men and women. A Christian parent has a real duty here and must perform it not only for his or her own sake, but for the present and future welfare of the children.

Laxity in nurturing in a child the vital elements of Christian character will offset the advantages of even the most diversified formal education. Some of the essentials that go to make up strength of character are endurance, strength, honesty, integrity, purity, stability, and sincerity. These virtues will enable any young person to weather the storms of life.

Stewardship of Children's Spare Time

There are entirely too many institutions, organizations, clubs, and places and modes of entertainment competing for the spare time of our children. All these distractions call the child away from the family circle. It is during their spare time that children get into trouble and young adults fall into many temptations. Too many children spend too much time away from home in unsupervised activity or staring stupified at a hypnotic and tasteless TV show.

During three months out of each year, neither the public nor parochial school reaches the child. Although technically under parental supervision at that time, if the home does not provide something to occupy a child's time, he or she will be under the tutelage of others. Sometimes these "others" are a poor influence and will lead a child astray. Even a group of "good children" must not be left alone for long periods of unstructured playtime.

Schoolteachers take children through studies that lead through high school and to college or other advanced training. Citizens pay taxes to support the teachers and facilities for this service, but a major part of "education" is not obtained from books or formal teaching. The Christian home must supply this essential ingredient. Christian parents will save themselves from many heartaches and their children from many pitfalls if they will pay careful attention to monitoring how their children spend leisure hours and suggest activities that are both enjoyable and morally acceptable.

The Church and the Children

Establishing stewardship habits in children will tie them to the church. Once in place, such habits develop a personal sense of responsibility in young people, keep the church in touch with its youth, encourage them to attend morning worship, help increase the present and future income of the church, and underscore the joy and pleasure of being a church member. Giving is an act of worship, and children therefore gain personal satisfaction and a rich spiritual experience in placing their contributions in the Lord's treasury.

What are some of the best-of-everything gifts that Christian parents owe to their children? What could be better than the following?

1. A good name, which God's Word says is better than great riches (Prov. 22:1).
2. A clean, healthy body.
3. The best possible education. Any nation whose adults ride in automobiles and fly in airplanes should not permit its children to walk in ignorance.
4. The ability and desire to do an honest day's work for an honest day's pay.
5. A good example of moral behavior.
6. Christian training at home and in the church.
7. Instructions regarding the use and abuse of money.

Stewards in the Community

Every citizen either raises or lowers the moral tenor of the city in which he or she resides. So, too, does every church member add to or detract from the influence of the church in that city. No one can be part of a community without having some effect, and the influence can be either good or bad. Christian stewardship requires that every believer actively participate in community life and add a strong influence on the side of righteousness.

One cannot read the Pauline Epistles without being impressed with the thought that Christians are to be noticed in a community because of the difference Christ makes in their lives. The apostle wrote: "For we are unto God a sweet savour of Christ, in them that are saved, and in them that perish" (2 Cor. 2:15). If there is to be any fragrance of Christ in the wicked metropolis, only individual Christians are able to supply that fragrance. Christ is the beautiful lily of the valley, the refreshing Rose of Sharon, and those permeated with the Savior's essence will become obvious in a community because of the positive influence they dispense.

Christians must shake themselves loose from the sophistication, profanities, and secular obsessions of this world. On the day of Pentecost, Peter challenged his listeners to save themselves, and this challenge continues with us today. The Christian influence we have in our communities says to the unsaved today: "Save yourselves by coming to Christ."

Advertising for the Best

A momentous tide of materialism is engulfing our nation. Even some Christians are being swamped by the deceitfulness of riches. Advertisers budget huge sums to convince us that a fulfilling life can be built upon gadgets, high fashion, cosmetics, glamor—and pills, drinks, and tobacco. In the face of widespread immoralities and obscenities, it becomes the responsibility of every Christian to place on display the gospel of Jesus.

An unselfish and thoughtful personal ministry furnishes the best advertising for the Lord. People see the work of the church in their community wherever Christians minister to the needy, care for the sick, love the unlovely, help secure work for the unemployed, pray for the discouraged, lift up the fallen, and perform these services for everyone, regardless of their station or ethnic background. Service for the community will help the community know the church as billboards never can.

Community Service Speaks

Much indifference could be changed to interest if all the people in a community believed that preachers and church members were interested in every individual, home, farm, township and business around them. Children, youth, and adults can help their pastor in his or her efforts to make the community experience a "religion" that is inseparable from the general activities of everyday life.

Stewardship means that Christians are to use their

Stewards in the Community

natural talents and training in outreach to others. For example, a nurse who is proficient in dealing with the diseases that arise from unsanitary conditions, and who knows what can be done on an individual basis to help save those who live in poverty, could prove of invaluable assistance to a pastor. Helpless thousands who live in homes where ignorance and slovenliness have fostered disease call loudly for such a volunteer worker.

Just as it has become fairly commonplace for medical and legal professionals to "reach out and touch someone" by volunteering their expertise on behalf of the indigent, there are many ways any Christian can practice a ministry of service within the community. A carpenter might spend some Saturdays helping elderly neighbors with home-repair projects they can no longer handle themselves. Or a personnel manager might visit the local schools to provide job-hunting advice for teens who have little hope of affording advanced studies. The opportunities to serve are limited only by one's imagination and desire! God needs people in every legitimate walk of life to help him carry on his work here on earth. Personal contact between the "unsaved" and the Spirit-filled Christian is worth far more than can be estimated in advancing kingdom principles.

Every church should have a wide-awake and efficient publicity committee composed of men and women selected for their ability to do this special "advertising for Christ." In the ideal situation, the chairperson should be someone familiar with the business of promotion and advertising. Monthly meetings should be held for planning, discussion, and progress reports. Church officials should place in the hands of this committee a specified amount of money to be used for the sole purpose of making the church known in the community. An alternate plan would be for the pastor to select qualified persons to assist with the advertising program on a more informal basis.

Checklist for Publicity

The following list shows some of the ways to "advertise" the church's services and thus solidify fellowship within the congregation and clarify its goals for the community at large:

1. Edit and publish a monthly church magazine that carries a pastoral message, news about the church, and items of general interest.
2. Edit and publish the weekly bulletin. (In churches where the pastor does not have a paid assistant, volunteers can help with this task.)
3. Write up appropriate church events as general news releases. Some such publicity is carried in many newspapers without cost to the church. However, a newspaper may limit the amount of free coverage. If advertising space must be purchased, the cost may be prohibitive, but there are many items of interest a newspaper would be happy to receive. Check out the guidelines your local newspaper follows. Some of the things that could be publicized are a ground-breaking ceremony or dedication of a new sanctuary or education building, special conventions attended, outstanding guest speakers, and death of a faithful church servant.
4. The publicity committee should arrange with the pastor and lay leaders to have special sermon series or important days in church life advertised in attractive style. Those handling such paid notices should be constantly studying new and ingenious media techniques.

5. Place church notices in public places. Every hotel and railroad or bus station in the community should have a neat, nicely framed card listing services and church activities to which the public is invited.
   6. Spot announcements on radio and television programs are used successfully by businesses and community organizations. Announcements of church activities can be used with equal effectiveness.

The church has many good products—and they are free! These products should be placed on display so as to let the community know that the church has something they need and would also enjoy having.

Public Servants to All

The rugged road from Jerusalem to Jericho was twenty miles long, and along that somewhat lonely distance it descended thirteen hundred feet. In biblical times, the road was not only desolate, rocky, and hazardous, it was infested with robbers.

A lawyer, in asking Jesus a question, "Who is my neighbor?" received a very strange answer in the form of a parable (Luke 10:25–37). Jesus did not tell the story of the good Samaritan for the sake of focusing on the neighbor in need, that poor wretch who had fallen among thieves. Jesus gave us that parable to describe the real neighbor, that one who went far beyond the line of duty in showing mercy on the unfortunate "stranger."

The amount of the Samaritan's charity was not large —only his time and enough money to compensate the innkeeper for a few days' lodging. But it was indicative of the generosity of the caregiver's mind and heart. It did not matter who the unfortunate man was, where he had come from, where he was heading, or what he was going to do when he got there. Here was simply someone who needed help *now*!

This illustration shows that the Master interpreted discipleship at least partly in terms of generosity. The true follower of Christ will not stop to count the cost of serving others. Rather, a disciple is a steward who continually lives and gives and serves beyond the limits that might be expected by the world at large. On that basis, Mary anointed the feet of Jesus with a costly box of ointment (John 12:3), and anyone forced to go with another for one mile was called upon to go two (Matt. 5:41).

Serving School Organizations

Although the church is to be the great center of moral education, other institutions share this function in varying degrees. Basic religious training is primarily a work of the home, supplemented by the church, whereas "reading, writing, and arithmetic" are generally considered the domain of the school system (whether public or church-related). However, to the extent that a teacher's value system and opinions can color the so-called facts of history, social studies, and even "pure science," morality and religion *are* taught in all schools.

Christ told his church to make disciples of the world, which includes training men and women for "religious service," as broadly defined. This implies more than just church membership. All Christians who do their lifework well and with due regard for the welfare of others are actually earning high grades in religious studies.

The public school that teaches children to read and write is indirectly serving as a unit of the church! Without the ability to know and understand the contents of the Word of God, no Christian could reach full spiritual

Stewards in the Community

maturity. How difficult it would be to search out the divine truths contained in God's Word if we did not have the ability to read it. In this and other learning areas, Christian parents should take an active interest. Working with school organizations will bring better mutual understanding as to how the educational system can best serve young people's needs.

Serving on the Community Level

One of the questions that looms large in the minds of many Christians is, "Where and how shall the church secure new recruits?" Jesus said, "The field is the world . . ." (Matt. 13:38). Farther than the eye can see, and no matter where one goes on this earth, there is a field of humanity in which to work for spiritual harvests. In every city and town, Christian laborers have been sowing seed for over nineteen hundred years. The Lord tells us that the fields are ready, white unto harvest (John 4:35). Happy is the one who with faith in God and a wholesome attitude toward mankind steps into a field, confidently swings God's scythe of truth, and gathers another sheaf, to replenish the church's forces and release her sustaining power in the world.

The area in and around a local church can be particularly fruitful. In a church where the Spirit of God has been applying his truth very directly, the people in the congregation are usually most responsive. But adjacent to the church, in the same community, is fertile ground—a seedbed for the Lord. Probably at no other time can a church official meet as many business and political leaders than in the civic meetings of the secular community. Local organizations may informally help (or hinder) the church by their ability and willingness to mention a fund-raising campaign, grant special building variances and permits, or endorse a nondenominational evangelistic effort. Securing the goodwill of such groups helps assure the church of their more direct cooperation when needed.

Being a Christian "Everywhere"

Observers both within and outside the church are often rather free in expressing their opinions about why church members bother to attend public worship services. For some parishioners, these critics suggest, church membership is "fashionable" in the community, or perhaps pressure has been brought to bear upon them by friends or business associates. The eloquence of a particular preacher attracts others, as does the entertainment value of a fine organist and choir. Some people simply like a gathering place in which to model their new clothes and hairstyles. Ambitious businesspeople find church services a fruitful source of potential customers, and the socially-conscious may hope to achieve popularity with a particular group or meet newcomers for selfish reasons.

However, untold numbers of God-fearing people attend church for more legitimate and commendable reasons. Primarily, of course, the Bible commands believers to come together in worship and praise of the Lord. Since worship and service go together naturally in the eyes of God—in fact, they are inseparable—many attend church for the highest motive of all: to serve.

Christians are to be Christians *everywhere*. This is perhaps an overworked statement, but it is true nonetheless. Can someone be a Christian at church while being a cheat at business, a liar in the community, or an angel of darkness at home? Of course not! A Christian's life must proclaim faith in God in *everything* he or she does and says. Nothing is more impressive to others than a believer's daily walk as a child of God. That, too, is a ministry of high importance.

The Church *as* a Community

In the records of the formation of the early church, no statement is more significant than the one found in Acts 2:44: "And all that believed were together, and had all things common." *The Living Bible* reads: "And all the believers met together constantly and shared everything with each other." Each Christian congregation is an association of people who are united in spirit and who therefore aim to represent ideal community relationships.

History records that the nineteenth century was marked by many great discoveries and wide-sweeping social movements, especially in America. One of the greatest movements was formed for and among young people. In 1881, a few young people met with their pastor in Portland, Maine, and inaugurated the Christian Endeavor Movement. From this small beginning has sprung a network of organizations among the young, some even reaching small children. That illustrates a far-reaching community of spirit.

When our pioneer forefathers planted the Stars and Stripes in previously unexplored western territories, they had risked life and limb on the journey to their new homes. Anyone starting across the Plains Country alone was committing gradual suicide. What sane man would expect to survive attacks by wild animals, or by Indians protecting their lands, and the deprivation of water or food along the way? Without proper direction, a lone traveler could wander aimlessly for months, but—by combining forces and strength—untold wagon trains successfully made the trip. So, too, must the church be a community that combines the strengths of many individuals to fight worldly dangers, including selfishness, corruption, greed, and faithlessness. The church universal is *in* the world, though not *of* the world.

A Community Within a Community

The church, on both the worldwide and local levels, is a community with a definite and specific ideal—the Christian life. The church finds its boundaries within a larger community that does not profess to maintain the same standards. Although part of the common stock of humanity, the church is committed to the gospel of Jesus and what it implies about proper living. It is true that the church should be separate from the world's evil, but never from its people. Christians should be insulated, but not isolated.

A Christian is a public person, the instrument by which God's purposes of universal mercy are to be accomplished. Christian life is interwoven into a system of benevolences. Neither is a believer's death excluded: "For whether we live, we live unto the Lord; and whether we die, we die unto the Lord: whether we live, therefore, or die, we are the Lord's" (Rom. 14:8). This sentiment is strikingly characteristic of Christianity and marks it with features noble and gracious. If the church community does an effective job for God, it will add worth and goodwill to the secular community.

The Church's mission is not to draw people from the community to itself, as if to build an exclusive ecclesiastical club.

That kind of "elitist" approach would leave the larger community to degenerate and decay. Rather, the church must outfit itself to serve the entire community with righteousness and goodness. The underlying purpose is

Stewards in the Community

to make every community a social body in which the ideals of Jesus Christ are accepted and where his Spirit is actualized. The ultimate success of the church may be measured by its loyalty to the local community's economic, social, and moral needs.

The united body of Christ has a divine mission. Failure of the church to bring its guiding principles to the lives of the people around it in every possible way is disloyalty to Christ. Jesus never sent hungry people away. He blessed the bread and blessed the fish and gave the massed crowd something to eat. It would be impossible for a church to have a positive overall influence if its members in effect told a starving man that it would nourish his soul but refuse to feed his hungry body.

Since the church is clearly an organization that follows divine leadership, its services are essentially and fundamentally "religious." That is, the church is expected to bring the community into vital touch with God through his Son Jesus Christ, as does no other organization in the world. This by no means implies that the church's services to the larger community should be limited to prayer and preaching, singing and shouting, or even open invitations to church-sponsored dinners, picnics, Bible study, and other such programs. Instead since every human need presents an opportunity to serve, the church body will be continually interested in municipal concerns—in lawmaking, education, and relieving human suffering wherever it is located. In fact, the church will vigorously pursue every avenue in uplifting human life. This most people-oriented of organizations is to spread its gifts throughout the entire local community, thus demonstrating its divine origin and purpose.

The increasing number of civic service organizations now available might tend to convince even avowed Christians to divide their loyalty—to put their trust partially in secular agencies rather than totally in God's provision. But true wisdom will call for coordinating the work of private and state facilities with church-related instruments of service. The church is the most important social organization in any community because its outreach is unlimited and its effects are eternal. The church, too, must use human minds and hands to accomplish its aims, but its practical methodology must be such that "the law of the spirit of life in Christ Jesus" fits it naturally.

A vital church has a structure and plan for action that will perpetuate and nurture its existence and spread its influence through the world. As the apostle Paul observed: "From whom the whole body fitly joined together and compacted that which every joint supplieth, according to the effectual working to the measure of every part, maketh increase of the body unto the edifying of itself in love" (Eph. 4:16).

Service Specifics

A church best serves the community—its own and the larger one in which it exists—when it is well informed about all the citizens of that community. To this end, every congregation should be kept informed about such matters as the number of people in the area who are without a church connection, the denominational affiliation of present or potential church members, the location of children not enrolled in Sunday school, housing and other economic conditions needing correction, the names of civic leaders and directors of school programs, and any other data that might be helpful in its work. For example, a church might organize a survey crew to canvass the community every two years and thus gather information that might be used in a membership drive.

Stewards in the Community

A Christian should regularly be trying to win new souls to Christ. That broad goal also includes helping every fellow believer find a church home.

Any activity of the church that is conducted in a reverent and conscientious manner is just as "Christian" as a prayer meeting or a Sunday school class. Every phase of church work is a religious act of praise when done in the spirit of love. It is possible that the implementation of properly motivated plans be done in such a way that selfishness surfaces. Then the life of the church will be demoralized. But it is more probable that the Spirit of Christ will prevail in all church matters, making them a means of grace to the whole Christian family. A church can be truly effective only if it organizes its affairs on God-ordained principles and assigns sound leadership to advance the work of the Lord Jesus. Not all soulwinning is accomplished through revival meetings or mission service on foreign soil.

For anyone realizing that the church knows the way to eternal life, it is sobering to think of the great responsibility laid on the church to give this light to all mankind. Only the church possesses what the world really needs! People everywhere want "happiness," but many know not what the word means. They want life; they want a thrill; they are searching for something to satisfy their wants as well as their needs. The church of Christ offers all this and more, but the church must display its goods and make known how to obtain what it has to offer. This can only be done if the church "advertises" its services. Any money budgeted for regular, systematic, and attractive promotional purposes is well spent.

A visiting minister once said, "If you want your merchandise bought, put it out on the shelf where the people can see it. Very little will be sold from under the counter." Ultimately, the best advertisement for the church is its faithful stewards: "Ye are the light of the world. A city that is set on a hill cannot be hid. . . . Let your light so shine before men, that they may see your good works, and glorify your Father, which is in heaven" (Matt. 5:14, 16).

10

Stewards in the World

The apostle Paul consistently displayed great genius and zeal while establishing churches in the metropolitan areas of his day. His strategy never required more brilliance than it did in Ephesus, the most influential metropolis in Western Asia at the time. Because of its strategic location on the most direct route between Rome and the eastern provinces, Ephesus was a commercially rich city and population center of that end of the Mediterranean seaway.

One cannot read Paul's letter to the church at Ephesus—or, for that matter, New Testament accounts of other early Christians—without feeling that these religious pioneers were driven by a powerful inner force that caused them to think in universal terms. In accounts of Paul's missionary journeys, as well as in his Epistles, the apostle seems always in a hurry to take his message to another city. In writing to the church at Rome, Paul revealed his profound sense of obligation to every man on the face of the earth who had not yet heard the good news of forgiveness from God through his Son Jesus. Paul wanted all mankind to know that this forgiveness was available to anyone who asked. Christian stewards in the world today should have the same attitude as Paul—a consuming desire to take the gospel to every living person.

The Family of Nations

In Christian civilization and for eons before, the family has been the fundamental unit of society. Unquestionably, this family unit forms a field for Christian service of unequalled fertility and potential. All mankind is a family, too. People of every race and nation and from every station and walk of life are members of this world family—the human family that God created and sent his Son to rescue from the effects of sin. Everything God made and placed on the earth has always done exactly what God put it here to do except his most prized creation: mankind.

When Paul wrote to the church at Ephesus, he obviously had in mind the world's family of nations: "For this cause I bow my knees unto the Father of our Lord Jesus Christ, Of whom the whole family in heaven and earth is named" (Eph. 3:14–15). Similarly, Paul preached to the Athenians: "And [God] hath made of one blood all nations of men for to dwell on all the face of the earth . . ." (Acts 17:26).

One of the most interesting developments in modern scientific agriculture is the way wasteland can be turned into productive soil. Some scientists declare that hundreds of millions of acres of barren soil can be "born-again" and made as productive as the fertile fields of the Mississippi Valley, simply by adding the right ingredients. On a human level, the main purpose of the coming of Jesus was to restore fallen humanity by providing the right ingredient—himself. Once more we could all be proper children of God.

The Family Ideal

Just as every earthly father has some ideals in mind for his loved ones at home, without doubt the heavenly

Stewards in the World

Father has set standards of excellence for *his* family, whose "home" is the world. This is essentially a matter of defining relationships. First, God would have us think, feel, and behave as if we are his children, which means that we are to love God as the very Source of our being, praise him in thankfulness, and respect him in obedience. Second, we are to think, feel, and behave as if all people are our brethren. These two principles summarize the character, spirit, and ministry that make an ideal family unit—whether within the confines of a household or in the unbounded world around us. People in the family of nations who live by these standards learn to do God's will above their own and also to treat their fellowmen as loving brothers and sisters.

As the hero in a story illustrating the universal "good neighbor" principle, Jesus chose a Samaritan, a member of an ethnic group abhorrent to the Jews. He was a "good" Samaritan because he ministered to the needs of a fellowman whom representatives of the law and the church had passed by. He went far beyond the expected, for he paid the victim's hotel bill and provided an open expense account by promising to pay whatever was necessary to get the stranger back on his feet.

Where does "giving" actually begin? It begins with love: "For God so *loved* the world that he *gave* . . ." (John 3:16). This, as Paul reminded us, is also where Jesus began: ". . . who *loved* me, and *gave* himself for me" (Gal. 2:20). A cup of cold water given in his name, Jesus indicated, is the same as giving it to him. Acts of loving God and acts of loving one's neighbor can hardly be separated. In this twentieth century, whether it be in Jerusalem or Dallas, Moscow or Little Rock, this principle still works miracles.

One has only to look around or read the daily newspaper to see that conditions in the world are far from ideal. There is limited consciousness of (and love for) the Father and his ways. And there is scarcely an abundance of active brotherly love among men as they deal with one another! Before we as Christians take a stand that will hurt or discourage another or destroy that person's status, we should think in terms of brotherhood. How would we act if this were a member of our immediate family?

The church of the Lord Jesus Christ has the one Great Commission in the world, this being above and beyond all others—to seek first the kingdom of God. We in the church are to bring all men to Christ that they may join the family of God and come to know the Father. Establishing this relationship will create in all men a desire to do the Father's will and make secure their determination to adopt every principle that is essential to the growth of his kingdom. The church must emphasize the necessity for the spiritual union of man with God, for humanity is capable of true brotherhood *only* through the Spirit of Christ. The man who *loves* those in his home *serves* those in his home. And those who love God will love and serve all others in God's kingdom.

The Governing Principles of Love Gifts

"Alabaster money" is a gift to God that is not a regular offering or tithe. The amount given is not linked to dues, requirements, regulations, assessments, or budgets of any kind. Like Mary's costly perfume, it is something we might like to have for ourselves—leisure time, personal possessions, and such—but we give it to the Lord instead. A true gift or act of service is never made by reluctant hands or an indifferent heart. God's reward for giving is administered when the voice of love speaks

Stewards in the World

louder than the voice of duty. Let us examine the areas in which acts of Christian love count most:

1. *Protection.* Loving brothers and sisters, without being coerced, have a keen sense of responsibility about protecting each other from harm. Therefore, Christians must try to protect fellow members of the family of God from the powers of evil.

2. *Consolation.* Recognizing the many kinds of physical suffering and emotional pain in the world and helping to alleviate them were matters of great concern to our Lord and Master while he walked on earth. We, too, must do all we can to ease the sufferings of our brothers and sisters in God's family.

3. *Education.* Professionals in the field of education generally agree that their responsibility includes training youth to be of service in the community and world. Christians help toward that goal by teaching youngsters to be valuable to the kingdom of God, to fill their minds with that which is pure, clean, holy, and right. The apostle Paul wrote: "Finally, brethren, whatsoever things are true . . . honest . . . just . . . pure . . . lovely . . . of good report; if there be any virtue, and if there be any praise, think on these things" (Phil. 4:8).

4. *Exemplifying Morality.* Merely passing stern judgment on an erring fellow member of the family of God both fails to meet the underlying needs of the sinner and shirks one's own responsibility to the church universal. Setting an example of what is morally correct, while speaking loving instruction about avoiding what is morally wrong, will do far more good for humanity than "stone casting" by self-appointed judges in ecclesiastical courtrooms of their own making.

5. *Promoting Good Health.* Practically speaking alone, preventing disease processes is highly preferable

to curing them, since keeping a body healthy is far more constructive (and usually less costly) than being rescued from a painful or debilitating malady. On a more spiritual level, does not the Word of God endorse proper health care? Members of the family of God are reminded that Jesus Christ offered himself as a living sacrifice to God, undefiled, "holy and without blemish" (Eph. 5:27), on our behalf. Following that example, Christians can do no less than take care of their bodies, which, as we know, are temples of the Holy Spirit (1 Cor. 6:19).

6. *Fighting Vice.* Almost every city today (and even some rural communities) has a vice commission to deal with the poisonous effects of the immorality and self-destructive habits underwritten by money-hungry crime lords. It is as though a powerful toxin is spreading in our midst, preying mainly on the weakest members among us. If a rattlesnake bit a child, we would hardly choose to ignore the incident. Ideally, we would not only extract the venom as quickly as possible but would destroy the snake and others of its kind. Christians should be the first in any community to promote a program that will eliminate carnality and corruption at all levels.

7. *Poverty Programs.* Will the poor always be with us, as Jesus said? (Matt. 26:11). It is probably true that there will always be poverty, at least until the kingdom of God is fully actualized. But one glaring contradiction facing us involves the vast resources of wealth and plenty on one hand and, on the other, the millions of people worldwide who go to bed homeless and/or hungry, night after night. If we are ever to deal with deprivation on a wide scale, we must start at the local level. Since pride and self-respect often make those in need reluctant about asking for help, we who are blessed with bounty should not wait to be asked.

The Bible poses a thought-provoking question: How

dwells the love of God in a man who "shutteth up his bowels of compassion" when he sees his brother in need? (1 John 3:17). When he was on earth, Jesus led all others of his community in caring for the poor. If there is one specific ministry most closely related to soul-winning, it is the caring for the needs of the body that houses the soul.

The Whole Gospel for the Whole World

When man first sinned against God, that sin justly called forth a divine curse on the human race from that time forward. God fixed the ultimate penalty for sin as death. At the same time, God's love for man appeared even more clearly than his wrathful judgment, for God proclaimed his intent to redeem sinful, fallen man. Later, at the birth of Christ, angels declared the glorious beginning of the prophecy's fulfillment: "For unto you is born this day in the city of David a Saviour, which is Christ the Lord" (Luke 2:11). Jesus himself affirmed the full scope of his ministry when he said that "the Son of Man came not to be ministered unto, but to minister, and to give his life a ransom for many" (Matt. 20:28). Paul repeated the same inspired message after Jesus had ascended to his Father: "This is a faithful saying, and worthy of all acceptation, that Christ Jesus came into the world to save sinners . . ." (1 Tim. 1:15).

Now this same gospel, the message of the saving grace of Jesus Christ, must be preached everywhere. This was not merely a request or a plea by Jesus. Rather it was a command: "Go ye therefore, and teach all nations . . ." (Matt. 28:19).

But the gospel does not end with the saving grace of Jesus. The whole world must know also of his great promise: the infilling of the Holy Spirit (Acts 1:4–5, 8; cf. John 16:7–16). On the day of Pentecost, Peter told those assembled that the Spirit would come to "you, and to your children, and to all that are afar off, even as many as the Lord our God shall call" (Acts 2:39). The saving grace of Jesus Christ and the baptism of the Holy Spirit give believers access to God's glorious blessings, which are distributed according to his infinite wisdom. There are gifts of the spirit operating in the lives of the baptized, and there is also the blessed privilege of trusting God for divine protection, for "with his stripes we are healed" (Isa. 53:5; cf. 1 Peter 2:24).

Jesus did not leave his disciples hopeless in the world and without kingdom glory to anticipate, for he promised to return: "I will come again" (John 14:3). The church of the Lord Jesus Christ is looking forward with blessed hope to the soon-return of the Savior. ". . . it is high time to awake out of sleep," said Paul, "for now is our salvation nearer than when we believed" (Rom. 13:11). Christ shall not only return to this earth to claim us as his bride, but eventually he shall set up his kingdom here on earth. Then righteousness shall rule the nations.

The above summary does not exhaust "the whole gospel," but mentions only some of its major points. In preaching the *whole* gospel to the *whole* world, we must declare the Word of God in all its fullness and glory.

Who Shall Go?

It is not the responsibility of a local church to select certain individuals of the congregation and inform them that they are the ones to forsake friends and home to take the gospel message to the ends of the earth! First of all, an evangelist must be someone with personal knowledge of Christ's saving grace. It seems logical that those who would tell someone else about salvation should have no doubts about whether they themselves have been "saved." Only those with a real experience of salvation should take to the mission field. Second, those who go should be dedicated Christians with a consuming desire to carry the message of hope wherever God leads them. People who have "nothing else to do" or just want to "take a trip" are responding to the idea of glamor and adventure and have no business bothering the cause of Christ with their kind of halfhearted service.

Who Shall Prepare Them?

Through the years, the ministry available in Christian schools has had a glorious history. Throngs of earnest young men and women have entered their doors, eager to serve, but woefully unprepared. Such young people usually feel the hand of God on their lives but are unsure of the direction he wants them to take. After abiding for a while within a Bible-oriented school and under the constant touch of cultured and consecrated teachers, they came forth as polished diamonds, destined to adorn the crown of the King. Only then is it fitting for them to bear the blessings of their ministries to earth's countless multitudes.

Christian schools represent an investment from which the world at large is continually realizing invaluable returns. Church-oriented schools are indispensable. Without them, where would future spiritual leaders be trained to guide people through their ever-increasing mental and spiritual difficulties? Yet, in this age of doubt and skepticism, there are many nay-sayers who would discount sacred truth, debauch purity, and dethrone God. The champions of righteousness must therefore be strong-willed, hearty, and fully armed for the battle against evil.

Obviously, a person must be prepared for the specific career or other goal he or she wishes to pursue. If a young man wants to be a successful farmer or rancher today, he would attend agricultural school. Would-be attorneys aim for law school; doctors need medical-school training. Studying electrical engineering would no more prepare one for a nursing career than art courses would lead to a degree in dentistry. So, too, do those who wish to serve in the mission fields need adequate preparation in a Bible-based college and/or seminary. Education for Christian service is one topic rarely found in secular training centers.

Who Shall Send Them?

It becomes the solemn responsibility of every born-again believer who is not able (or willing) to carry the gospel far afield, to help send those who can. Some may be able to give to the cause more than others, but this does not eliminate the responsibility of those who have only small amounts to give. It is not a matter of "feeling generous" or giving simply because the worker is going out from the local church. It is an obligation—a way of fulfilling the Great Commission to take the gospel to the ends of the earth. God calls on each of his children to participate in evangelism, both directly and by support of all those who carry the salvation message.

What Are The Rewards?

What Christian—for the sake of a few thousand or even a few million dollars—would suggest closing the door of salvation? Who would deny young people the privilege of preparing themselves for one of life's most sacred tasks—taking the message of light and life to a waiting world? Who would want to accept the responsibility of withholding the life-renewing gospel from scores of souls? Yet that is exactly what happens each time a Christian refuses to give, pray, consecrate, dedicate, prepare, or go! Rewards will be great, "joy unspeakable and full of glory" (1 Peter 3:8), when at last a countless throng of blood-washed saints stands around the throne eternal, giving praise to God Almighty for everlasting life. It will be worth it all when we see Jesus!

All Life Is a Stewardship

Paul admonished that "ye present your bodies as a living sacrifice . . ." (Rom. 12:1). Although many studies on the subject of stewardship deal only with tangible substance, "stewardship" applied only to material possessions does not fulfill the word's entire meaning. Being one of God's stewards means that we dedicate ourselves completely—possessions, power, possibilities—everything that goes to make up total living. Certainly "life" would be considered man's most valuable possession. What would *you* give in exchange for your life? There have been those who would have given everything they possess, the value running into millions of dollars, just to live a while longer. Eternity is priceless, yet God's grace makes it free for the asking.

Early Christians did not act as if their lives belonged to themselves. For example, when Peter and John were arrested and brought before the Jewish leaders, these fervent new Christians felt there was only one thing for them to do: continue speaking God's message of salvation (Acts 4:1-20). They had determined to live only for the glory of God regardless of the consequences. The possible cost did not enter into their decision. It was a matter of total service to Christ. Their lives belonged to him and they would therefore take his message to the world. Jesus will supply whatever any of his servants need, according to his sovereign will.

Paul's Surrender to God

Where a moral issue is at stake, an unseen divine presence is at work to guide the Christian's mind. There is an active Spirit-filled energy streaming from God to man, and the most dangerous attitude anyone could take would be refusing to do whatever this inner persuasion was commanding. When God lays a sense of responsibility on us, he is dealing directly with us as individuals. When this duty becomes perfectly plain, we have come to a crossroad in our spiritual walk and must choose either obedience or disobedience.

Sometimes the call to God's service is dramatic and life-changing, as it was when Saul—later Paul—walked the Damascus Road two thousand years ago. It seems no small wonder that a great, strong, bright light shone round about Saul, persecutor of Christians, to mark his conversion experience. This was probably an indication of what it would take to break through his prejudice and hatred of the new believers. Though blinded on that fateful trip, Paul saw his unfairness to those he had persecuted. He recognized the blackness of his own sinful past and was ready to dedicate the whole of his born-again life for service. He asked, "Lord, what wilt thou have me to do?" (Acts 9:6). Here was a prominent man with a well-trained mind, willing to be a bond-slave of Jesus; a man of position and culture, ready to be a servant; a man of authority, a man of culture standing at attention saluting his Captain. This is the full life! This is the good life! This is the life of a steward! All for Christ and Christ for all!